CONSULTATIVE SELLING™
Seventh Edition

CONSULTATIVE SELLING™

Seventh Edition

The Hanan Formula for High-Margin Sales at High Levels

Mack Hanan

American Management Association
New York • Atlanta • Brussels • Chicago • Mexico City • San Francisco
Shanghai • Tokyo • Toronto • Washington, D.C.

Special discounts on bulk quantities of AMACOM
books are available to corporations, professional
associations, and other organizations. For details,
contact Special Sales Department, AMACOM,
an imprint of AMA Publications, a division of
American Management Association,
1601 Broadway, New York, NY 10019.
Tel.: 212-903-8316. Fax: 212-903-8083

This publication is designed to provide accurate and authoritative
information in regard to the subject matter covered. It is sold
with the understanding that the publisher is not engaged in ren-
dering legal, accounting, or other professional service. If legal ad-
vice or other expert assistance is required, the services of a
competent professional person should be sought.

Library of Congress Cataloging-in-Publication Data

Hanan, Mack.
    Consultative selling : the Hanan formula for high-margin sales at
high levels / Mack Hanan.—7th ed.
        p.   cm.
    Includes bibliographical references and index.
    ISBN 0-8144-7215-X
    1. Selling.   2. Selling—Key accounts.   I. Title.

HF5438.25.H345   2003
658.85—dc22

                                                            2003019604

Consultative Selling℠, Profit Improvement Proposal℠ and its acronym PIP℠,
and PIPWARE℠ are registered trademarks of Mack Hanan.

Printing number

10   9   8   7   6   5   4   3   2   1

To my partners,
James Cribbin
and
Herman Heiser,
who set out with me on a mission to convert the sales function into a delivery system of continuous new value for its customers, and who, along the way, enriched me with the value of their refusal to settle for anything less than the continuous improvement of our own standard of performance.

CONTENTS

CONTENTS

A Personal Note
from the Author

Chief executives who used to ask me, "What do I need you for?" have learned that they need me to equip their sales forces with an answer to that same question when it is asked by their own customers that will give them a compelling reason to buy.

In an era when customers control the way they want to be sold and, by doing so, have superseded their suppliers' pretensions of account control; when products and services, however new, are likely to enter their markets as instant commodities; when margins are the reward for improving a customer's profits rather than for improving your products or services; either you never leave home without new competitive advantages to bring to a customer or you stay in the car.

Customer managers at all levels, even technically trained managers in R&D, engineering, and IT, are getting smarter about their businesses, not just their technologies. In the words of one chief information officer (CIO): "When one of our typical suppliers comes in, it's always some account manager with a classic product-based pitch. That's their comfort zone. They're just not prepared to say, 'Let's talk about where your business is going, and here's how we can help you meet your goals.' Maybe their top management can talk this way, but I never see them. They never see me either, so they have no concept of what my management is telling me I have to start paying attention to. Somebody says, 'He's in technology, so go talk technology to him.' But that's not really where I'm at anymore."

Today's account managers—no longer Arthur Miller's road warrior, who was "out there with a suitcase and a smile"—carry improved profits, not products, in their bag. Theirs is not the gift of gab but the greatest gift of all, being able to help customers grow their business so the consultative seller's business can be grown by high-margin sales in return.

Even at the time of this book's first edition in 1970, creeping commoditization was already in hot pursuit of proprietary brands. Sales representatives were already sounding alike, on the way to becoming commodities themselves. Price lists were already bargaining chips. Customers were already looking for help from their suppliers to make their businesses more competitive, but not many of their suppliers were listening; they were preoccupied with protesting to customers why each supplier was better than the others. Venting had become nine-tenths of vending.

The pioneers who were the first to put their hands in mine had the market all to themselves for improving customer profits. Phil Smith partnered with Oscar Mayer around a value proposition that opened up the packaging of their new product portfolio to his Continental Can Company in spite of duplicative competition with commodity processes and prices. Paula Brown partnered with United Technologies around a value proposition that opened up their telecommunications networks to her AT&T in spite of obsolescent technology and higher prices.

Bill Franklin and John Malone pushed and pulled their engineering-obsessed company, Hewlett-Packard, into proposing business values instead of operating specifications. Kevin Howell made sales history by closing a $1.25 million agreement in the midst of a Consultative Selling training program where his Digital Equipment account team and their customer manager were learning together how to partner in profit improvement. Danielle Buth goes on year after year being Salesperson of the Month at Siemens by reducing her small-to-midsize manufacturing customers' costs and increasing their revenues a little more each time she walks in their doors. GiGi McDougall comes away with a million-dollar-plus agreement from Microsoft for her Storage Technology System after a single six-hour-meeting—a rate of almost $167,000 per hour.

The Smiths, Browns, Franklins, Malones, Kearneys, Howells,

Buths, and McDougalls of the world of Consultative Selling keep their eyes on the eagle: their customers. They never see their competitors who keep their eyes on each other and mutter medieval mantras about "killing the competition." For every sign on the walls at Hewlett-Packard that read "Kill DEC," there was an equal and opposite sign at DEC that read "Kill H-P." Meanwhile, their customer midlevel operating managers, whose names they did not even know and whose problems and opportunities were enigmas wrapped in mysteries, were looking in vain for help to avoid being killed by their own competitors.

The power of Consultative Selling to compel customer awareness, positive attitude, and acceptance has been proven over and over again by companies as diverse in size, industry, and nationality as Asea Brown Boveri and Zytron.

Lew Platt, the former CEO of Hewlett-Packard, liked to talk about the challenges that faced H-P and what H-P was doing about them because he thought that it built credibility with customers. Let's talk about you, he was apt to say. What do you think about "the H-P way" of reducing inventory? The way we're reducing receivables? The way we're reducing product design cycles? The way we're reducing manufacturing costs?

Platt envisioned H-P as "a functional, generic commodity business." When people challenged him with what twenty-five words he would use to describe H-P, he could do it in only two: measure and compute, without encumbering them further with a third word about their added value.

As far back as the 1960s, Tom Watson Jr. was restructuring IBM so it could become its customers' profit-improving consultant. "We make computers," Watson used to say, "but we sell customer growth by applying them." In many cases, Watson was able to prove that IBM could grow its customers more cost-effectively than they were growing themselves. A dollar invested with IBM, he went around telling customers, can yield a greater rate of return than the same dollar invested in your own operations. Then he would set about to quantify it.

Watson's competitors, meanwhile, had invented every reason in the world not to replicate his strategy:

- "We call on a wide range of contacts within our customer base: purchasing agents, technical staffs, business managers, and others. We like to think that we have access to multiple contacts at multiple levels throughout our customers' organizations. But in a practical sense, we spend more time with the technical groups and end up selling to the purchasers."

- "Our customers are very well aware of our manufacturing costs and how they impact our product costs. We can justify price increases only if raw material costs increase or market conditions change. Regardless of any value-added services we try to associate with our products, our customers still know what the price of the product is, and that's all they will pay us for."

- "Our sales reps are making an average of 400 calls a year. That stretches them very thin. They know they're on a treadmill of discounting their values away, but they don't have the time to get off it and do anything else. If they try, our customers' purchasing agents do everything they can to discourage them, which includes threats to stop doing business."

- "The best return we have been able to get for our investment in value-added services is the right of first refusal, which doesn't cost our customers anything the way paying us a price premium would."

I once walked into a conference room where a sign entitled "Why We Are Different" was on the wall. It read, "Compugen's services are differentiated from our competitors by the caliber of our people and the flexibility of our processes." It was signed "Gerry Skipwith."

I wrote my own sign on the whiteboard underneath it and signed it "Mack Hanan." "Compugen's customers are differentiated from their competitors by the caliber of their profits and the competitive advantage of their processes."

The top sign was before Consultative Selling; the bottom sign was after.

Mack Hanan

PREFACE

Consultative Selling is the delivery system for value. In return for improved customer outcomes, Consultative Selling delivers improved margins back to you.

- Instead of sitting across from a purchasing manager—or a manager of information services or telecommunications who has a purchasing role—consultative sellers sit side by side with a midlevel operating manager who runs a profit-centered line of business or a cost-centered business function.
- Instead of selling the added cost of a product, service, or system feature by feature and benefit by benefit on price and performance, consultative sellers sell the added value of an improved contribution to profits.
- Instead of asking for money, they offer money in the form of a return on their customer's investment.
- Instead of a spec sheet with line-item prices, they specify the value they can add on a costs and benefits analysis of line-item cost savings and revenue benefits.
- Instead of talking down their competitors, they talk up the enhanced competitive advantage customers can seize over their own competitors.
- Instead of paying lip service to the concept of partnership, they create the new streams of cash flow that pay their entry fee into true customer partnerships.
- Instead of professing added value, they propose it in quantified, time-framed terms, measuring it milestone by milestone, selling it, being evaluated on it, and being paid for it.

No wonder Ann Gessen's internal memo to her manager at Metaphor Computer Systems is typical of every seller's first date with Consultative Selling:

> I presented my first Profit Improvement Proposal yesterday—a preliminary PIP to a senior VP of operations to get his feedback before formally presenting to him and the other senior managers next week. He went nuts! "This stuff is great. I can't believe it. Your company is finally doing something right by relating to me as a business manager. I came in here dreading that you were going to give me a standard price-performance pitch. What a relief!" At that moment, all I wanted to do was to kiss Mack Hanan.

If Ann Gessen had been a vendor instead of a consultative seller, her customer would never have been able to share the opportunity she represented to make his operation more competitive. Only his dread, not his profits, would have been realized. Ann would have presented him with a "discussion document" or a "concept presentation," two forms of confessions of ignorance about the relationship of her customer's business and her own. Or, even more demeaning, she would have tried to sell him a "study." Discounting is the name of the luxury tax she would have had to pay for the enjoyment of her ignorance.

The Profit Improvement Proposal™ (PIP)™ is the original value proposition. All proposals that sell on ROI (return on investment) or that use a Cost-Benefit Analysis spreadsheet are derived from the PIP.

PIPs are conversion machines. They convert the operating benefits of a suppliers' technology into financial benefits for their customers. Because technology is supplier specific while financial benefits are the universal language of business, customer managers can immediately perceive what even the most exotic technology can contribute to their competitiveness in terms of saved operating costs and increased earnings from operations.

The PIP process focuses on adding value to a customer's cost centers by making them less costly to operate. It adds value to profit centers by making them more productive in generating revenues and enhancing their earnings.

In both of these respects, PIPs affect customers' variables: their variable costs and the elasticity of their revenues. PIP time frames are short term, circulating customers' capital fast and recirculating it as soon as possible through continuous PIPping.

PIPs measure their incremental value in dollars. As part of their conversion mechanism, they translate time into money.

Similarly, they monetize reduced labor intensity and increased manufacturing productivity. Customers' pounds of weight saved or the number of extra cases, gallons, or carloads shipped become their money equivalents in a PIP.

While PIPs are generally targeted to the improvement of profit contributions made by customers' tangible assets, PIPping works every bit as well with the intangibles. Dell Computer's build-to-order assembly system is regarded by consultative sellers as a cost reducer; they ask how its already low current costs can be further reduced. Wal-Mart's supply chain management system is also a cost reducer, showing up as everyday low prices in its stores. Consultative sellers ask how improved productivity in managing the chain of suppliers can yield an even lower cost base and thereby generate greater revenues.

The critical-to-success Internet management skills of amazon .com are revenue generators to consultative sellers, who set about to increase their moneymaking capabilities.

Consultative Selling makes more money for you than vending because it generates new high-margin sales volume that vending would never have been able to bring in. These incremental flows of new cash dollars into your business have a greater net worth to you because they can be achieved at lower selling costs than vending.

Figure P-1 shows the 10-year composite before-and-after Consultative Selling norms of an information technology product line according to five key performance indicators: average margin, length of sales cycle, average annual revenue per sales representative, average dollar value per sale, and revenue-to-investment ratio per sales representative.

Figure P-1. Before/after norms for Consultative Selling.

Key Performance Indicator	Before Consultative Selling	After Consultative Selling
Average Margin	0.80	350.0
Length of Sales Cycle	365 days	90 days
Average Annual Revenue per Sales Rep	$1.5M	$4.5M
Average $ Value per Sale	$300,000	$1.25M
Revenue to Investment Ratio per Sales Rep	5:1	100:1

Consultative Selling works equally well for public sector customers whose businesses are nonprofit or not-for-profit.

Vending ignorance ends and Consultative Selling wisdom begins when sales representatives put their first Profit Improvement Proposal—in front of a customer manager and begin to sharpen up the PIP's problem or opportunity diagnosis, firm up its prescription for an optimal solution, and close the proposal by going upstairs for funds.

Consultative Selling's three strategies of positioning you as a value-adder, proposing the financial value you can add, and partnering with a customer manager to comanage the realization of the value are designed to take you through the PIP cycle in minimal time with a maximum hit ratio. If you use PIPWARE™ software*—the Profit Improvement Proposal on a Disc—you cut your time outlay even more. The minimal time to complete a PIP is less than a minute. Each additional iteration takes another sixty seconds.

When you partner with a customer manager through the intermediary of a Profit Improvement Proposal in PIPWARE form,

---

*Profit Improvement Proposal™, its acronym PIP™, and PIPWARE™ are registered trademarks of the author. PIPWARE is the computer software that enables the Internet- and corporate intranet-accessible Consultative Selling e•xpert xystem™ training program.

your proposal is no longer yours alone. Realtime customer inputs make it "ours," a partnered business case in which the customer becomes preinvested in the joint creation of the solution as the first step to his or her investment in its funding. As a result, the hit ratio from PIPping is almost always one to one. Why not? With your help, customers end up proposing to themselves.

Mosaix is a manager of customer telecommunications services. "For many years," its people say, "Mosaix won deals with superior technology. Our salespeople focused on selling product—great product, but product. We got into pricing wars. We claimed technological superiority. Competitors claimed technological superiority. Customers were confused. Our win rate declined to one win in ten bids."

Realization dawned: compete on value, by making positive contributions to reduce customer costs and improve revenues. Mosaix experimented with Consultative Selling. "The performance of our consultative sellers eclipsed the product sellers with eight high-margin wins out of every ten."

In addition to preserving margins and increasing the win rate, Consultative Selling proved to have another advantage for Mosaix. "It kept out competitors."

As Mosaix discovered, Consultative Selling restructures the entire vendor sales process:

- It redefines the product from representing a material or piece of equipment or a packaged good to represent *profits.*
- It removes price from representing the cost of products, services, or systems and repositions it as the *investment* required to realize an added value.
- It redefines competition from representing a supplier's rivals to consisting of a customer's current *costs* or *sales revenue* targets.
- It repositions the supplier's core capability from creating improved products or services to creating *improved profits for customers.*
- It redefines the customer from a Box 3 techno-purchaser to a *Box 2 line of business or business function manager.*
- It redefines the seller from vendor to *consultant* and redefines the customer to a *client.*

The advent of Consultative Selling made vending on price and performance the default strategy for B2B (business to business) sales. Product-centered selling was left to suppliers who did not know their applied value and so could not price or sell it. It remained as the fallback for suppliers who were content to sell commodities instead of brands, who believed that they could make up for discounted margins by more and more volume, and who were dedicated to killing their competitors rather than creating killer apps to grow their customers.

Consultative Selling's critical success factor is its ability to free price from cost and competition by relating price to an investment. In this way, it can be compared to the value of new profits that are to be improved by the seller—in other words, it can be compared to its return instead of to its cost or performance.

By altering the unit of sale from a product to an improvement in profits, Consultative Selling changes the basis on which sales are made. All sales are the result of comparison. Vendor sales compare competitive products on the basis of their price and performance. Consultative sellers compare a customer's current operating performance with a future improvement. They differentiate themselves by selling the difference.

In this way, Consultative Selling enables account managers to pull off the "hat trick" of selling:

1. Compel customers to increase their use of the seller's products or services.
2. Obtain a higher margin for it.
3. Provide customers with a higher return than by discounting price.

Initially conceived as a sales strategy, Consultative Selling has changed the terms and conditions of competition, the supplier relationships of customers, and the organization structures of the companies that practice it: not just in expected operations such as marketing support and customer input into R&D (research and development), but also in the forms of virtual organizations with spun-out or outsourced sales forces and the two-tier sales force model with a top tier composed of consultative sellers dedicated to key account customers and a bottom tier of third-party resellers, telemarketers, and retailers.

Outsourcing, facility management and category management, networking, systems integration, and process re-engineering would all be impossible to propose, evaluate, or finance without Consultative Selling.

The consultative seller's added value lies in his or her ability to apply intellectual capital to an otherwise physical capital proposal and thereby add value to it. Physical capital is a commodity. Only the value added by intellectual capital is brandable, which means that it alone is capable of commanding margin. Intellectual capital is the intensely personal possession of each consultative seller. Ultimately, it is the seller's differentiator. It allows one seller to prescribe a solution that returns $1.50 for each customer dollar invested while another seller can return only $1.00, with both of them using the same physical capital components.

As the contact point between suppliers and customers or providers and clients moves up the value chain from seller-buyer to comanager–manager, consultative sellers alone, of all supplier people, possess the mindset and skillset necessary to oversee their mutual growth. They are their customers' and clients' natural growth partners. As a result, they are their own companies' natural developers of continuous new streams of profitable sales volume.

With the advance of Consultative Selling into the next generation of business, consultative sellers are becoming the sole survivors of direct sales forces. Who needs vendors when all they do is discount price? Who can afford vendors when they add more to the cost of sales than they recover in margins? Who can justify vendors when customers publish requests for proposals on their Web sites or fax RFPs, circumventing human contact? And whom do vendors call on as customers outsource and downsize their purchasing functions?

Figure P-2 shows the advance of Consultative Selling as vendor sales forces are retrained to sell consultatively or are replaced by third-party resellers, telemarketers, cataloguers, and Internetters. From now on, the rule is clear: Whenever a human being adds his or her cost of labor to the sales process, only Consultative Selling can add back the value to pay for it and still make a profit.

Figure P-2. Advance of Consultative Selling.

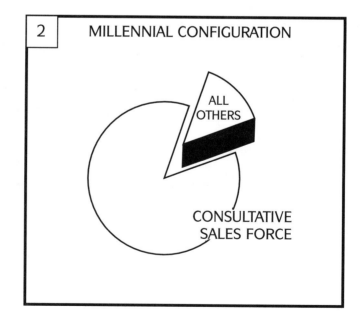

Consultative Selling was created to be the ultimate expression of one-to-one marketing: one Profit Improvement Proposal for an improved profit contribution by one application to one operation of one customer manager by one sales representative. Each PIP is one of a kind. It is application-specific, operation-specific in a specific industry, and customer manager-specific in its enhancement of one of the key performance indicators. It is also sales rep–specific. It comes out of each rep's individual mindset. Except by chance, no one else is likely to diagnose a customer problem or opportunity in exactly the same way, prescribe exactly the same return on the same investment within the same time frame. As much as Consultative Selling is single-customer marketing, it is also single-rep selling.

Consultative sellers who are doing their job should be able to point to improvements in customer operations to which their specific PIPs have been contributing:

- Is cash flow increasing in volume or coming in faster in a customer's line of business that has been PIPped? How valuable is the increase? What is the value added by faster inflow?
- Is working capital increasing? By how much? How soon after PIP implementation?
- Are receivables being collected faster? How valuable is the increase? By how much has the cost of collecting each dollar been reduced?
- Are same-day shipments increasing? By how many dollars' worth of goods? By how soon after PIP implementation?

In this way, Consultative Selling stands alone in contrast to the commoditization of products, services, and people in vendor selling. Suppliers and providers are branded by the differentiations of their PIPs. So are their customers. And so are their sales representatives and account managers, who become known by the contributions they make to the outcomes they affect.

Introduction

THE CONSULTATIVE SELLING MISSION

Consultative Selling is profit improvement selling. It is selling to high-level customer decision makers who are concerned with profit—indeed, who are responsible for it, measured by it, evaluated by it, and accountable for it. Consultative Selling is selling at high margins so that the profits you improve can be shared with you. High margins to high-level decision makers: This is the essence of Consultative Selling.

Since 1970, Consultative Selling has revolutionized key account sales. It has helped customer businesses grow and supplier businesses achieve new earnings along with them. Everywhere it is practiced, Consultative Selling replaces the traditional adversarial buyer-seller relationship with a win-win partnership in profit improvement. This is no mean feat. To accomplish it, Consultative Selling requires strategies that are totally divorced from vendor selling. It means that you stop selling products and services and start selling the impact they can make on customer businesses. Since this impact is primarily financial, selling consultatively means selling new profit dollars—not enhanced performance benefits or interactive systems, but the new profits they can add to each customer's bottom line.

The single most critical difference between Consultative Selling and vending is the way they deal with price. Vendors base price on their costs. Margin is their way of asserting the right to a "fair price." Consultative sellers base price on their value. They consider margin to be their responsibility, not their right. To them,

1

it is the sellers' responsibility to add sufficient value to customer businesses so that customers will be able to add margin to the sellers in return.

In this sense, margin is a consultative seller's pay for performance. The sale itself is no longer a transfer of a product or service in exchange for a price. It becomes a value exchange. In exchange for having their profits improved, customers trade off some of the improvement as margin to the supplier.

A consultative seller's price is a function of the contribution made to improve customer profits. The only way the seller can maximize price is to maximize the value of the profits that are improved. That requires the seller to stop selling products because there is no longer any way to make margin by selling the value of the seller's own assets. Margin can only be made by helping customers make their own assets more valuable.

Consultative Selling is selling a dollar advantage, not a product or process advantage. There is no way to compromise this mission. Anything less is vending.

Vending is discount selling, giving away value to make a sale. Discounting is taking on many forms that go far beyond price-cutting. Each of them represents another giveaway of margin that adds up to a hidden reduction in selling price:

- Multiyear contracts with built-in annual price cuts
- Zero inventory and just-in-time delivery
- Sharing in product development
- Free aftermarket services, such as training and maintenance
- Free upgrades
- Lease financing at below-market rates

Consultative Selling, on the other hand, is high-margin selling. Full margins are the proof of value. When they are discounted, that is proof that their value was not sold. The most frequent reasons are that it was not known or that it could not be proved.

Performance values put into a product or service are validated by the financial values a customer gets out of them. Performance values are important only insofar as they contribute to the value of a customer's operations—either they add the value of new or more profitable revenues or they help preserve that value by reducing or avoiding costs that would otherwise subtract from it.

Discounting denies that superior value has been put in or that superior value can be taken out—or, if it can, that it can be documented. With each discounted sale, value is either denied or downgraded. It is obvious how this deprives the seller of a proper reward. Less apparent, perhaps, is how their customers are also deprived. Unless they can know in advance what value to expect, which means how much new profit they will earn and how soon they will earn it, they cannot plan to put it to work at once. They incur opportunity cost even though they add value, because they cannot maximize it. Their own growth is impaired along with the growth of their supplier.

As long ago as the early 1970s, Bill Coors of the Adolph Coors Company said that "making the best beer we can make is no longer enough" of a value on which to base a premium price. Making the customer best in some way or other would be necessary to maintain the margins that were once easily justified by product quality alone. In 1977 a company named Vydec was finding it increasingly difficult even then to cost-justify its high-quality, high-priced information systems when competing against the decreasing costs of competitive systems. Its managers realized too late that the justification of a premium price could no longer be attributed to hardware performance. "Future hardware will all look alike," they admitted after the fact. "The greatest values will be in training, software, and system support. You will be able to almost give away the hardware."

COMPARING CONSULTATIVE SELLING TO VENDING

The differences between vending and Consultative Selling are significant. They are differences of 180 degrees. Their languages are different. Their mindsets are different. Their definitions of product, price, performance, customer—yes, even of selling—are different, as Figure I-1 shows. The main difference is in their ability to produce profits on sales.

Consultative Selling takes a position about the sales process.

Figure I-1. Consultative Selling versus vending.

Consultative Selling	*Vending*
The sellers supply profit as their product.	The sellers supply product.
The sellers offer a return on the customer's investment.	The sellers charge a price.
The sellers use a Profit Improvement Proposal.	The sellers use a bid.
The sellers quantify the benefits from their customers' investments.	The sellers attempt to justify their cost.
The sellers attach the investment to their customers' return.	The sellers attach a price to their product.
The sellers help their customer compete against the customers' competitors.	The sellers compete against their own competitors.
The sellers let their customers close.	The sellers try to close.
The sellers sell to a business manager.	The sellers sell to a purchasing manager.
The sellers feature their customers' improved performance.	The sellers feature their products' improved performance.
The sellers' products are improved customer profits.	The sellers' products are equipment, a service, a process, or a system.
The sellers sell vertically to a dedicated industry and to dedicated customers within it.	The sellers sell horizontally to all industries within a dedicated territory.

It says that there are two ways to sell. One is the way of outsiders, which is the way that most suppliers approach their customers. The customers' gatekeepers are their purchasing functions. At the gate, vendors who hope to sell high come face to face with gate-keepers who want to buy low. This is where sales cycles are born, costs of sale begin to accumulate, and margins are sacrificed. For every so-called coach, champion, or foxy politicizer who is cultivated at the gate, suppliers' costs of sale are being extended, their sales cycles stretched thin, and their eventual discounts deepened. Meanwhile, consultative sellers beyond the gate are extending customer budgets, stretching customer cash flow, and deepening their eventual profits. In the same customer worlds, these two strategies go on every day.

What separates them? They live by different rules:

- Vendor suppliers sell computers because they make them. Consultative sellers may make computers, but they sell the value they add by reducing a customer's downtime.
- Vendor suppliers sell packaging because they make it. Consultative sellers may make packaging products, but they sell the value they add by increasing customer revenues and reducing shipping costs.
- Vendor suppliers sell wireless telephone systems because they make them. Consultative sellers may make wireless telephone systems, but they sell the value they add by allocating manufacturing labor more cost-effectively.

No matter what vendor suppliers make, they sell it.

No matter what consultative sellers make, they sell the value it adds.

The essential differences between Consultative Selling and vending are made clear where value meets price at the point of sale:

- Vendors sell to buyers who want to minimize the prices they pay for operating assets. This requires vendors to sell against their competitors. Consultative sellers sell to operating managers who want to maximize the value they add to their assets. This allows consultative sellers to sell by comparing current customer outcomes to future outcomes that they propose to competitively advantage.

- Buyers want to reduce two types of direct costs: their costs of acquisition and ownership. Operating managers want to reduce the opportunity costs of delay in making their operations more competitive. This is why buyers can wait for a lower price while operating managers cannot wait for an added value.

- Buyers want to help reduce their suppliers' internal operating costs and share in the gains through reduced prices. Customer operating managers want to reduce their own internal costs and are willing to share in the gains from improved outcomes. This is why buyers try to control supplier operations while customer managers bring in consultative sellers to help control their own operations.

SELECTING CONSULTATIVE CHOICES

Selling offers practitioners three choices. If they make the right ones, they can maximize the earning power of their products and services. Before that can happen, they must first realize that the choices are available to them and, second, that the answers that lead to nontraditional profits and revenues are, themselves, nontraditional answers.

1. *What do you want to be compared with?* All selling provokes comparison. The traditional comparison positions one supplier's product as better. If you choose to make your customers compare your product features and benefits with those of a competitor, the customer will cancel out the similarities and devalue the differences by asking you to discount their worth. If the only difference is price, you will suffer fierce margin pressure.

On the other hand, you can choose another comparison. Instead of competing against the price of a rival supplier, you can compete against the current value that customers are receiving from one of their businesses or business functions that you can affect. If it is a cost center, what is its current contribution to cost? If it is a profit center, what is its current contribution to profits? In either case, the customer's current performance is your competition. Can you give them a competitive advantage by helping them differentiate themselves from their own competitors? This is what they try to do in their own business. If you can help them, you can sell them.

When you choose to make customers more competitive, you compete against their own rivals: their own costs that are unnecessarily high or their own revenues that are unnecessarily low.

2. *Where do you want to attach price?* Price is always "of something." The traditional object of price is a product or service. If you choose to attach your price to your product, the customer will compare it to the prices of competitive products. If your product is more similar than superior to them, or not sufficiently superior to make a difference, or is equal or inferior to its competitors, your price will be downgraded.

On the other hand, you can choose another attachment for price. Instead of inviting comparison with competitive prices, you can position your price as an investment and attach it to the customer's return. When the customer compares the return against the investment required to achieve it, the rate of return compares the productivity of investing with you against the rate of return from other incremental investments he or she is making all the time. The customer's investment performance is your competition. As long as you equal the hurdle rate for incremental investments, you represent an acceptable deal.

When you choose to make a customer more money, you become a supplier of funds. Your price, now no longer a cost but a returnable investment, can be directly compared against the return and is therefore freed from comparison with competitive product prices. Instead of having your price reduced, the customer may increase the investment if it will disproportionately increase the return.

3. *Whom do you want to make the decision?* There are two kinds of customer decision makers—purchasing managers who buy a product's price-performance, and business managers who

operate a cost center or profit center and who do not buy at all. Instead, they sell proposals to add value to the business line or function they manage, requesting funds from top managers to improve their contribution to profits.

The traditional buyers are cost-controllers. If you choose to confront them as your decision makers, they will faithfully negotiate away your margins in order to lower "the cost of goods bought." That is their job. Your relationship will be win-lose, and you will lose more than you win.

On the other hand, you can choose to partner with managers who act as your "economic sellers" inside their businesses, promoting your proposals to improve their contributions to profits. They compete for access to funds against all other managers; if they do not get funds, their operations cannot grow, nor can they grow along with them. They sell for you—actually, they sell for themselves, with your help—if you can add to the value of their proposals by allowing them to promise a greater return, a faster return, or a surer return.

If you make the three right choices, you are in position to compare your value against a customer's current value, attach your price in the form of an investment to your value, and partner with a business manager who sells your value. You are selling like a consultant.

MAKING THE THREE CONVERSIONS

Vendor sales representatives become consultative sellers by making three conversions in their mindsets:

1. They must convert price into investment. Price is a cost. As such, it has a negative value for which customers will pay as little as possible to obtain. On the other hand, investment connotes a return. Return on investment is a positive value. Customers put out money in order to receive a commensurate value in return.

2. They must convert a product or service into the dollar value that comes from being applied to a customer operation.

Consultative sellers sell the value added by application (VABA), not the product that is applied or the service that applies it. They are monetizers of their technology's performance, translating benefits like faster time to market or reduced downtime or speeded up cycle time into their dollar contributions to customer operating profits.

3. They must convert their focus on making individual stand-alone sales into making a portfolio of continuing sales, each one of which is a logical migration from its preceding sale. A customer's profit improvement cannot be a sporadic, periodic event. Instead, it must be an ongoing process whose continuous inflow of new streams of cash is predictable. Reliability of profit improvement is every consultative partnership's middle name.

The conversion of price into investment prepares a consultative seller to propose giving money to a customer rather than taking it away—to change what has traditionally been the cash outflow of a purchase decision into the cash inflow of an investment's payout.

The conversion of technical performance into financial performance defines the subject matter of sales consultation: improving customers' profitability so that their competitive advantage is enhanced.

The conversion of product-line sales management into profit-project portfolio management enables consultative sellers to integrate their mission with the customer operating managers who must become their partners. They plan long term; so must consultative sellers. They must grow their asset bases; so must the sellers. They are paid for their performance in maximizing the rate of return on the assets they employ; so must the sellers.

Whereas vendor sales representatives are exhorted to "move the iron," consultative sellers move money. They move customers' capital funds into investments. They move investments into returns. They move the return from each investment into a following investment. Like their customers, consultative sellers make money only when they keep it circulating in ways that add to its value. The three conversions they must undergo are required to maintain

9

money in motion. Idle money represents downtime. Profitless investments are the equivalents of scrap. Both take customer funds out of circulation, whereas investments in rapidly turning-over profitmaking proposals replenish funds, instill motivation to gainfully employ them, and assure consultative sellers of a perpetually prospective customer base.

Applying the Consultative Selling Process

Figure I-2 shows the four-part Consultative Selling process:*

1. It starts with a value database on the values you normally add to customer operations. Your normal values-added—your "norms"—are derived from the value database.
2. By comparing customer revenues and costs against your norms, a lead database is automatically created. A lead opportunity exists wherever your norms offer a competitive advantage over a customer's current performance.
3. Proposable leads flow into closable proposals. The outcomes from each closed proposal are fed back into the value database to fertilize your norms.
4. The process culminates with a partnered penetration plan that locks in your consultative partnership and locks out competition.

For many suppliers, such as manufacturers of components and subsystems to original equipment manufacturers (OEMs), Consultative Selling is their saving grace. Without it, they become vendors by default, as they stand by helplessly and watch their products disappear—and their margins along with them—inside their OEM customers' equipment.

"We are such a small part of the end product," they lament. "The user never sees us. Unless something goes wrong, he never knows we're there." Or "There must be hundreds of suppliers they

*Fast-Value Calculator™, Fast-Lead Targeter™, Fast-Close Proposer™, and Fast-Penetration Planner™ are modules of the Consultative Selling e•xpert xystem.

Figure I-2. Consultative Selling work flow.

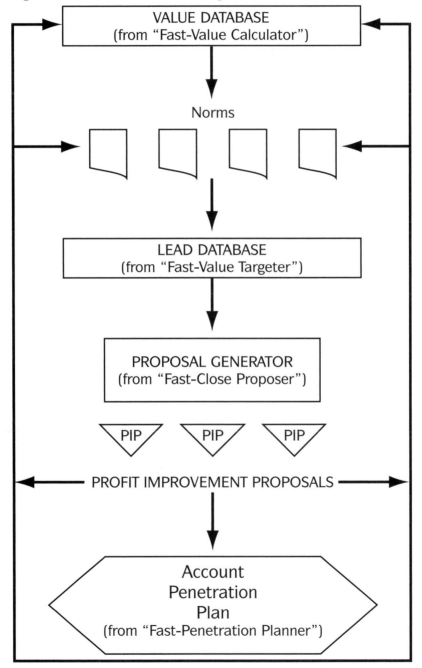

could buy from instead of us. If we try to raise our price, we're gone."

Honeywell Control Systems once said these same things. Then, applying Consultative Selling strategies, Honeywell has begun to quantify the added values they can bring. They have come up with a checklist of dollar-valuable benefits for their OEM customers, each one of which can form the basis for high-margin sales:

Customer Revenue Improvers

1. Faster new product start-up time
2. Improved product yield
3. Improved quality
4. Assured production scheduling

Customer Cost Savers

1. Reduced installation time
2. Reduced maintenance time
3. Reduced labor
4. Reduced process downtime

Honeywell has also prepared a checklist of added values that can be offered by OEMs to their own customers as a result of the contributions made by Honeywell's controls:

Customer's Customer Revenue Improvers

1. Product uniformity
2. Same-day order fulfillment
3. Longer term warranty
4. Reduced downtime

Customer's Customer Cost Savers

1. Reduced energy costs
2. Reduced manufacturing cycle costs
3. Reduced environmental penalties
4. Reduced costs of scrap and rework

Honeywell's controls still remain unseen unless there is trouble. But Honeywell's contributions to customer profits are now made immediately visible, before installation, on a PIPWARE cost-benefit analysis. By equipping its customers' sales forces with their own cost-benefit analyses and training them to sell consultatively, suppliers like Honeywell can help create cash flows that they would never otherwise be able to effect and can partner with their OEMs in sharing the benefits. "We can point to at least $65 million in increased business," says marketing VP Ralph Genesi, "and that's probably low."

The same strategy can be employed with dealers, distributors, and third-party value-added resellers (VARs). In this way, suppliers who are low on a value chain can extend their reach to end users to whom the value added is highest and whose gains are greatest.

CONDENSING THE SALES CYCLE

When you sell as a vendor, you invite the two-pronged costs of a drawn-out sales cycle. You incur the direct costs of selling over and over again until a sale is made or lost. Either way, you also incur opportunity cost. While you are waiting to close with one customer, you are delayed in starting up a new sales cycle with another. You pay this part of the price in lost opportunities or inflated costs for staff that could be smaller if it could be freed sooner to make the next sale.

Vendor sales cycles are unnecessarily prolonged because it is in the customer's interest to trade off time for the price cuts that inevitably accompany it. Consultative Selling makes time the customer's enemy. Delay works against the customer because it increases the opportunity cost of not improving profits day by day, week by week, and month by month. The longer the customer delays, the greater the cost. Once a revenue improvement or cost reduction is available, the customer must begin to flow it into operations or it is lost, either in whole or in part.

This internal pressure to improve profits provides customers with a strong incentive to close proposals. Each day's delay postpones payback of their investment and moves the eventual return on the investment at least one more day into the future. Because of the time value of money, each dollar they can obtain from working with you is worth more to them today than it will be worth tomorrow. If they have it today, they can invest it. By not having it until tomorrow, they sacrifice the value of both the principal and its interest.

By prolonging your sales cycle through vending, you sacrifice the contribution your own sales force can make to your profits. Assume that you currently have a twelve-month sales cycle, which is a common cycle in telecommunications and data processing system sales. Make the further assumption that each sales representative has an annual quota of $1.5 million and costs you $300,000 a year. If you can shorten the sales cycle by only one month through Consultative Selling, you can save $25,000 on the cost of each representative each year. The extra month of selling time will give you an incremental yearly gain of $125,000 in sales by each seller.

This adds up to a total improved contribution per representative of $150,000 a year. If ten representatives deliver the same incremental contribution, you will have achieved the equivalent contribution of one additional representative each year: $1.5 million that you will not have to spend a single dollar to realize. These virtual sales representatives are your most productive sellers because they generate only revenues, no costs.

Figure I-3 shows the Hewlett-Packard sales cycle, typical of vendors. The close takes place, if at all, at the end of eleven successive steps.

The origin of the time costs and direct costs in the H-P type of sales cycle are shown in Figure I-4. Line A-B represents the increasing direct costs of sales from a prolonged sales cycle. It also includes the opportunity costs of a delayed close that postpones the creation of a receivable. While these costs rise as the vendor sales cycle goes on, line C-D shows how the net present value (NPV) of the vendor's technology decreases over time, making it worth less when the customer finally decides to buy. The customer is being cheated of the supplier's value as well but is able to compensate for some of the loss by paying a lower price.

Applying a technology to add value to a customer business is

Figure I-3. Vendor sales cycle.

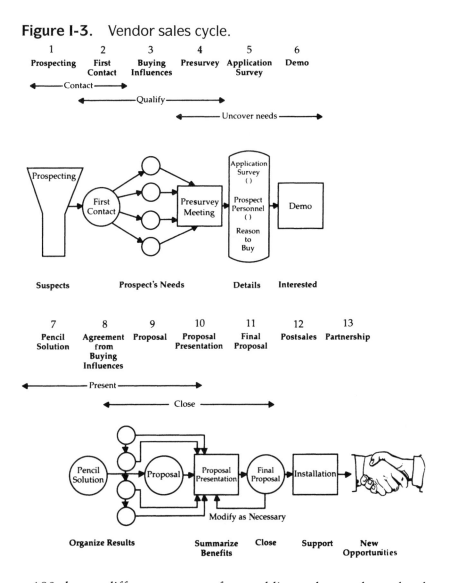

a 180-degree different strategy from adding value to the technology. When you claim that your technology can be an enabler of improved customer profitability, you take on two new responsibilities. First, you must know the customer business well enough to know how to enable it. Second, you must know how much of a contribution you can make to its current values and how soon you can make it.

Figure I-4. Vendor sales cycle costs.

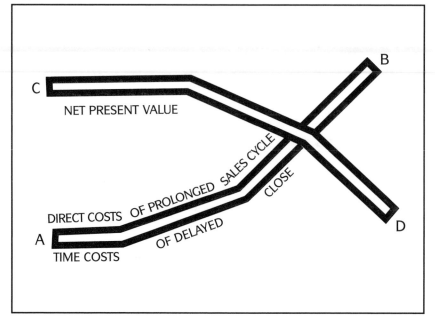

The second responsibility makes it necessary to learn how to convert technical values into economic values, in other words, to translate operating performance specifications into financial specifications.

The first responsibility introduces you to the customer's world of management acronyms:

• You have to know each customer manager's CSFs (critical success factors) that compose the 20 percent of all the factors that person must manage that contribute 80 percent or more to success.

• You have to know each customer manager's KPIs (key performance indicators) by which his or her success in managing the critical factors is measured and the objectives for improving them that each manager is tasked with. For each KPI you have to know the industry BOB (best of breed) or BP (best practice) against which your manager partners are being evaluated by their top managements.

• You have to know the EVA (economic value added) that each customer manager is currently contributing to total profits, and you have to learn the economic value you are able to contribute over and above the current EVA. This is your "product." Its value in dollars and time becomes the basis for your price.

MAKING YOURSELF THE NUMBER-ONE ASSET

The way customers determine their return on the investments they make when they buy from you is to divide their profits by the amount of the investment. This tells them whether they are going to come out with a net gain by doing business with you and, if they are, how much it is likely to be. It is up to you to tell them how you will make money for them. Will you help them increase their volume or their margins? Or will you help them reduce their operating costs? Or will you do both? If you can answer yes to any of these questions, you may be able to sell to them on the basis of your return instead of your cost.

Once you free yourself from being positioned as an added cost, customers will be able to regard you as an adder of value—an asset whose investment pays back a profit. The price that you ask them to pay to invest in the assets you want to sell to them can now be freed from being attached to the asset itself and can become related to the customers' return. By relating your price to your value as a profit contributor instead of to the performance features of your asset or to the prices of your competitors' assets, your price will be seen as an investment in a profit-making asset.

The V word—*value*—is the key word in Consultative Selling. Consultative sellers know their value, sell their value, position their value as their product, and price its value. They take pride in their value and are sure about their ability to deliver it to their customers. Their value is not in providing a service. Instead, their service is providing their value.

Consultative Selling makes "getting to close" predictable at a hit rate that is virtually one to one. There are two reasons why this is so: It compels buy-in on first proposal from customer managers who want to realize the full net present value (NPV) of a supplier's technology without incurring the opportunity cost of delay; and, just as it wins faster, it enables suppliers to lose faster and cut their losses as soon as they perceive, during preliminary proposal, insufficient partnerability on the part of a customer. This saves them the ongoing costs of making one cut after another, only to end up with discounted margins that can make a sale profitless, assuming it eventually takes place.

In these respects, not only is Consultative Selling the master quantifier of added values, but it is also the unfailing qualifier of opportune and inopportune selling situations.

PART I

POSITIONING AND PARTNERING TO PROPOSE HIGH-MARGIN VALUE PROPOSITIONS

CONSULTATIVE POSITIONING STRATEGIES

1

How to Become Consultative

In just three sentences you reveal whether you are a consultative sales representative.

In the first sentence, a consultant identifies a customer problem in financial terms—what the problem is costing the customer or what the customer could be earning without the problem. If you mention your product or service, you are vending and not consulting.

In the second sentence, a consultant quantifies a profit improvement solution to the problem. If you mention your product or service, you are vending and not consulting.

In the third sentence, a consultant takes a position as manager of a problem-solving project and accepts single-source responsibility for its performance. In the course of defining the project in terms of contribution to customer profit, you are able to mention products and services for the first time.

If you are selling as a consultant, it is easy to predict what the fourth sentence must be. It will be a proposal of partnership with your customer's managers in applying your system to solve the customer's problem.

A consultant's problem-solving approach to selling requires helping customers improve their profits, not persuading them to purchase products and services. To solve a customer's problem, a consultant must first know the needs that underlie it. Only when a customer's needs are known can the expertise, hardware, and services that compose a system become useful components of their solutions. This is the difference between servicing a product and servicing a customer. It allows your relationships with customers to be consultative rather than the simple sell-and-bill relationship that characterizes traditional customer-supplier transactions at the vendor level.

The ideal positioning for a consultative seller is *customer profit improver.* You can achieve this position by affecting one of a customer's operating processes in two ways: reducing its contribution to cost or increasing its contribution to sales revenues. A consultative seller's primary identification with profit improvement rather than with products, equipment, services, or even systems themselves gives the sales approach an economic objective. It focuses attention on the ultimate end benefit of a sale, not its components or cost. This gives you the same profit-improvement positioning as your customer has. It also professionalizes your mission by expressing it in business management terms, not sales talk.

SELLING RETURN ON INVESTMENT

From a customer's point of view, a consultative sales representative is an integral part of every sale. Unlike product vendors, who are identified as a part of their own company and therefore do not go along with the sale of their product or service, consultative sellers are embedded in their systems and are "packaged" along with them. Although a piece of equipment may endure longer than the equipment vendor does, the consultative seller generally goes on making an important contribution to customer profit long after the original system has been installed. The seller's durability with a customer aptly defines the vital role a seller plays over and above the other elements of a consultative system.

A consultative sale is not the sale of products or equipment. Nor is it the gift of so-called "value-added services," which are actually cost-added services, since their dollar value added to customer operations is almost always unknown and their cost is almost always unrecoverable by attempts to price them. A consultative sale is the sale of a positive return on the customer's investment: the economic impact of what is sold and not the components of the sale itself.

The most difficult challenge to consultative sellers is to stop selling products and start selling the added financial values that they can contribute to a customer's business. This requires more than merely substituting one vocabulary for another; it means substituting one mindset for another. Before this can be done, however, you must first undergo a desensitization to traditional product affiliations.

Most sales representatives metamorphose into consultants through a two-stage process. The first stage is to forsake performance benefit orientation for financial benefit orientation. This is akin to the classic features-versus-benefits conversion that all vendors undergo. It is the next order of magnitude. But in Consultative Selling, performance benefits are insufficient reasons for a customer to buy. Performance benefits describe what a product *is;* they are its operating specifications. Consultative Selling requires a seller to describe what a product *does;* these are its financial specifications. It is the end accomplishment of a product's performance benefits that must be sold.

The second stage in translating performance benefits to financial benefits is the calculation of their dollar values. These values, referred to as *incremental profits,* are the consultative seller's stock in trade.

Product desensitization starts with awareness that systems selling is a translated dialogue. All systems components, including the systems seller, must be translated into a customer value. Hanging out a laundry list of systems components is meaningless unless their individual contribution to the customer's incremental profit is quantified. Mentioning product, elaborating on the technological superiority of equipment, extolling its construction characteristics or other qualities—all are meaningless unless their incremental contribution to the system's capability for profit improvement is quantified.

Translating product performance benefits into incremental profit benefits is the way consultants must think. "What is the contribution to customer profit?" is their key question. They sensitize themselves to bottom-line thinking because they have learned that intermediate-line thinking fails to accomplish two key objectives: to position their customers as clients, since a client is a bottom-line beneficiary; and to position themselves as consultants, since a consultant is a supplier of bottom-line benefits.

Nothing will deposition a seller from a consultative stance faster or more certainly than lapsing back to a preoccupation with the product. It is the consultative seller's deadliest sin and an ever-present pitfall. At a customer's top tier, it can be fatal. The word *product* rather than *profit* lies poised from long habit on the tips of most vendors' tongues, ready to undo them. The best way to avoid slips of the tongue is to learn to use the new frame of reference in parallel with the old one and translate as you go. Whenever a product is mentioned, define it immediately in terms of its contribution to customer profit. This is what customers do; they listen for the numbers. Consultative sellers must become sensitive to this need and deliver the benefit that customers seek: quantification of the dollar values they will receive, not enumeration of the products or their performance specifications.

TALKING MONEY

In order to consult with customer operating managers on how they can improve their contribution to profits from an investment they make with you—in something you may call your "solution"—you must counsel with them in their own terms. These are not the vendor's terms of product features and benefits or price and performance. They are, instead, the basic language of business management in its most elementary form: Business Management 101.

At the customer manager level, "business-ese" is the only language spoken. It is transaction talk, the language of money being transacted. It is charged with action verbs: funds being *invested*, investments being *returned*, cash *flowing*, payback *occurring*, profits *improving*, costs being *reduced*, revenues being *increased*, and market share being *gained*. But these are simply ways of expressing what is happening to the subjects of these verbs, the dollars themselves. Customer manager talk is money talk.

What do you have to know in order to "talk money" well enough to be conversant in "business-ese?" There are two requirements: to know how money is classified and to know a customer's current money base of costs and revenues and how much you can affect them.

Classifying Money

Money is classified into six major categories:

1. *Investment*—what customers pay out.
2. *Return*—what they get back on what they pay out. The rate of return is the ratio of return to the investment.
3. *Payback*—when they get their investment back.
4. *Net profit*—what they make on their investment or their increment over and above payback.
5. *Cost*—an investment on which there is no return.
6. *Opportunity cost*—the profit they could have made on a different investment.

Analyzing the Customer Money Base

Consultants ask for incremental investments, money that is over and above the basic fixed-cost investments in the business as a whole. In return, they propose incremental profits. Incremental investments are discretionary. Customers choose among them on the basis of the best combination of muchness, soonness, and sureness that meets their needs.

Most consultative sellers propose incremental profit improvement. The rate of return is calculated only on the incremental investment in the proposal, which tends to make it exceedingly high. The customer's total investment in the business as a whole, or its total corporate return, is irrelevant. Consultative Selling takes place in the arena of a customer's microeconomics.

For that reason, the customer's balance sheet and income statement are neither causes nor effects of Consultative Selling. They will rarely, if ever, suggest leads. Equally rarely will they be impacted by a consultative seller's incremental improvement of any one business manager's contribution to profits. Yet, for the individual business manager whose profits are improved, the consultant's contribution can be a matter of life or death.

The consultant's micro impact makes a customer's annual report and 10-K interesting background reading but generally unproductive in targeting leads for Profit Improvement Proposals.

While it is true that all improved contributions to corporate profits flow to the corporate bottom line, they cannot be found there in annual or quarterly reports. In businesses of medium size on up, incremental profit improvements are subsumed in total profits. This makes annual or quarterly reports worthless as scorecards. For the same reason, they are also worth very little as lead targeters. Even when individual lines of business are broken out separately, the breakouts are almost always too large to be able to identify operation-specific cost problems or revenue opportunities for PIPping.

As background for operation-specific lead targeting, only the income statement offers anything of value. It shows whether profits are going up or down. The president's letter tells you the official reasons why. It may also indicate corporate priorities into which you can tie a PIP's business fit.

The income statement also lets you learn if total earnings are growing by giving you the information to calculate profit margins. If you divide annual net income by annual sales for the past three years, you can see if margins are shrinking even if sales volume has been rising. This tells you that business is being bought rather than sold and that your profit improvement projects must be structured to help restore income.

If you divide the cost of goods sold by total sales, you may see additional evidence that profit improvement is needed if cost as a percent of sales has been rising over the past three years.

The ability to interpret an annual or quarterly report's data, more so than the data itself, is a key resource. When a customer announces an earnings gain of 15 percent, it is easy to see it as a growth company. But if you compare the rate of earnings growth to revenue growth, you may see that earnings are growing faster than revenues. If so, earnings are coming from cost management, especially cost-of-sales management, and not from sales. The challenge to grow the top line, which is the key performance indicator of a growth company, is going unmet.

If you want to predict how likely it is that top-line growth will increase in the short term, you can try to estimate the short-term growth potential of current sources of revenue. In the case of Hewlett-Packard, most of its growth revenues are from low-margin products like personal computers and printers that are subject to continuing price erosion. If H-P's market continues to shift to lower-priced models, both revenues and earnings growth will come under increasing pressure.

The data you need to qualify and quantify a customer's consultative needs cannot be found in reports. It is business-line–specific and business-function–specific and consists of two categories of data:

1. In a profit-centered line of business, what contributions to its revenues and earnings being made by its critical products and services can you affect? What is the gap between the current contribution of a product or service and the line managers' objective to increase it? Can you help them close the gap enough to make you a compelling partner?

2. In a cost-centered business function, what are the current contributions to the function's costs being made by its critical factors that you can affect? What is the gap between the current contribution of a factor and the function managers' objective to reduce it? Can you help them close the gap enough to make you a compelling partner?

When you know the answers to these questions, you will be ready for your first conversation in "business-ese" with a customer manager. Your objective will be to reposition both of you: your customer into a client and yourself into a consultant.

MOVING THE DELTAS

Businesses traditionally focus on moving tons, barrels, cases, and carloads. When they become consultative sellers, they move

29

the deltas—the differences between the improvement they can contribute to a customer's costs or revenues and their current amounts.

Consultative Selling is a strategy of incremental business improvement, delta by delta, over the commercial life of a customer partnership. Each PIP proposes an added delta, which is its product.

If a customer's current cost of carrying inventory is $2.5 million a year and a PIP proposes to reduce it to $2.0 million, the consultative seller's product is the delta of $0.5 million in savings. If a customer's current sales are $10 million and a PIP proposes to increase them to $15 million, the seller's product is the delta of $5 million of new revenues.

Each successive PIP must be tasked to improve the incremental gains of its predecessors. In this way, a customer's business improvement can be continuous, and that business's consultative sellers will never be out of work.

The incremental nature of consultative sales also affects customer investments. For the purposes of cost-benefit analysis, a customer whose current cost of sales is $100 million and who invests $5 million to reduce them is incurring an incremental cost of only the $5 million that is chargeable to the consultative seller. The customer is not liable for the total current cost; the seller's responsibility is to make the incremental investment of $5 million reduce the cost of sales more than it adds to it.

Defining a *delta* as an increment is not meant to minimize it. Deltas that are too small may not be considered compelling enough for a customer to fund. The return involved may not be worth the investment, even if if is only a little one that will be at risk for a short time. Nor may a small investment be worth allocating a manager's time against it.

On the other hand, blockbuster deltas that encompass several increments at once may not be considered credible or, if they are believed, manageable. Very few customer managers are experienced in realizing rates of return of several hundred percent.

Suppliers' deltas are their differentiators. Their cumulative average becomes the suppliers' norms. When they are repetitively achieved over time, they brand the suppliers' offerings by quantifying their value. Not only does this set them apart from the competition, but it also positions the suppliers' business in their markets. They come across as the number one or also-ran cost reducer or revenue gainer for the operations and lines of business to which they are dedicated.

In Consultative Selling terms, customer relationship management (CRM) is the management of a continuous stream of deltas moved into a customer's operations. No matter how many other ways suppliers relate to their customers, improving customer profits is the single most important transaction that can occur between them. All else is parsley around the steak.

NORMING YOUR VALUE

When you average your added values on an application-per-operation–per-industry basis, you come out with your *norm* for your ability to add value to that operation in that industry with that application: your *normal value*. A norm is the composite of your consultative expertise in improving customer profits. Consultative sellers who sell from their norms are routinely able to say provocative things to their customers:

"According to our norms for the optimal layout for a print shop of your volume and type of production," 3M can say, "your current layout is depriving you of up to $1 million in profits every twelve months of operation."

"According to our norms for an optimal receivables collection system for food processors," AT&T can say, "you can improve the profit contribution of your current system by an average of $500,000 a year."

Norms are the consultative penetration tool. All consulting professionals work from norms, whose metrics represent their track record—their single most important possession and the foundation of their reputation. When their norms are the industry standard, they can use them to issue a "norm challenge" against a customer's current norms as well as competitive norms. The challenge develops leads. Here is the standard of performance for this critical success factor in this business function or business line, it says. *How do you compare?* If my norms are better than yours, ask me *how* I can bring you closer.

IBM sales representatives apply their norm templates to the manufacturing operations of pharmaceuticals makers like this:

> Our model design for automating a process like yours can help you reduce up to $200,000 in labor. According to our norms, your manning is excessive by five workers. Your control process is also slower than our standard in spotting and alerting you to deviations from specification. This will be reflected in added costs for quality assurance, scrap, and downtime. You can avoid these costs by computerizing your product testing and quality assurance. The difference between our models in these areas and your operations can yield you up to three quarters of a million dollars in the first year.

Unless you know the norms that a customer manager uses to make decisions and address them head-on in your PIPs, you can never achieve a one-to-one acceptance ratio of PIPs proposed to PIPs closed. Airbus learned this lesson when it came to Bob Crandall, when he was CEO of American Airlines, to propose a purchase of its 600-passenger jet based on a lower cost per seat mile than the Boeing 747. Crandall never looked at the Airbus cost-benefit analysis. Because he rejected the criterion on which it was based, it was irrelevant whether or not its numbers added up. "Big planes pay off only when they fly full," he said. "People don't want to get into an airplane that has 600 people and go to a place where they have to stand in line for two hours to get through customs." As a result, he concluded that "the fact that it's cheaper to fly per seat doesn't make any difference. The real cost is how much it costs per passenger."

Airbus may turn out to be more accurate than Crandall in assessing the market for big planes. It makes no difference. Crandall may be wrong about cost per passenger being more important than cost per seat. It makes no difference. As long as Crandall's key performance norm is cost per passenger, that is where—and only where—he will look for a signal to buy.

Your norms announce what is special about you: You know how to improve the profits of certain types of business operations. You know the standard specifications of what their profit values can be for these business functions; indeed, you are probably the discoverer and maker of many of them. If customers already exceed your norms, you can help them maintain competitive superiority. If your norms are better than a customer's current performance, you can help bring the customer up to your standard values.

Your norms—not your products—must become your consultative stock in trade. You sell consultatively by superimposing them over the current norms of customer businesses. A customer's new product norm may be only a plan. It does not matter. The plan contains a pro forma financial projection of the business-to-be. This is its *as-if* norm: as if it were up and running. Your norm is an *if-then* model: *If* the customer adopts your solution, *then* the customer norm more nearly approaches your own. The customer becomes improved.

At any given time, you can assess your competitive advantage as a consultative seller—in other words, the value of the net profits you normally contribute to your customers—by checking out your norms according to three criteria:

1. *Are they better than enough customers' current performance?* If so, you will have continued proposal opportunity.
2. *Are they better than your customers' industry average performance?* If so, you may have a competitive advantage over other consultative sellers to bring customers up past their industry average.
3. *Are they better than or as good as each customer industry's best practices?* If so, your norms are the industry standard of performance for all customers who want to achieve best practices.

Templating Proposable Leads

A consultative seller's database must be compartmentalized into three modules that he or she can scan left to right to target proposable leads:

Our Norm	Industry Average Norm	Customer's Current Norm

For the seller, Our Norm must be better than Industry Average Norm in order to be the norm leader. Our Norm must also be better than the Customer's Current Norm performance in order to have a proposal opportunity, either to improve customers to the level of industry average or to bring them closer to "our norm."

Norms give a consultative seller the vocabulary to speak in business-ese like this:

- Our Norm for average cost of recordkeeping of purchase orders, inventory reconciliation, and other related transactions in your product category is X dollars. Your cost is three times higher than our norm.
- Our Norm for average sales per square foot in your product category is X dollars. Your sales are five times lower than our norm.
- Our Norm for out-of-stock in your product category is X times per quarter. Your out-of-stock is six times greater than our norm.

Using norms, a consultative seller can get a handle on a customer's perception of the values that can be added by conducting challenging dialogs like these:

- "It takes you 3.0 hours to complete a design cycle. Our norm is 1.7. What is the value to you in costs saved and faster revenues for every 30 minutes we can bring you closer to our norm?"
- "It takes you 72 minutes to make a die changeover. Our norm is 46. What is the value to you in costs saved and faster revenues for every 10 minutes we can bring you closer to our norm?"
- "It takes you 3.6 years to introduce a new model. Our norm is 2.9. What is the value to you in costs saved and faster revenues for every 30 days we can bring you closer to our norm?"

Your norms are your value metrics. They say that there is a better way than the one the customer is currently practicing. The profit difference between the customer's way and your norm represents your added value. If you can enable a customer's new product, for example, to enter its market one month earlier than its plan, the dollar value of that month's earnings and the advance of one month in achieving payback of the product's funding represent your added value.

The first thing that you should propose to a customer is your norm for the customer's business or business function. "If your operation can more closely approach my norm," you can say, "some or all of the added value representing the difference between them can be yours."

What you do not ask is as important as what you do ask. You do not ask, "Do you want my product, service, or system?" Nor do you ask, "Do you want my solution?" or "Do you want to buy from me?" You need only ask whether the customers want their operation to approximate your norms more closely. When you ask that question, you are proposing to sell in a consultative manner. When the customers ask *how* they can make their operation come closer to your norm, they have begun to "buy" from you.

As soon as you know your normal benefit on an application-per-function or application-per-operation or per-process basis—they are all ways of saying the same thing—you can use it in two ways:

1. To target leads fast in customer operations where the current revenue performance is below the level of your norms or where the current cost performance is above them.
2. To get to proposal fast by presenting a preliminary benefit that can bring the customers' current performance closer to your norms.

You want to be able to say something like this to command a customer manager's attention:

We are experienced in improving the contribution to profits made by your operation. Our norms show that managers who implement our solution can increase their revenue contribution or decrease their cost contribution by approximately $x within y period of time. How do these norms compare with your current performance? If performing closer to our norms can make you more competitive, what if we can work together the way we are proposing to achieve a $000 minimum improvement within the next 00 months?

Creating Norm Warehouses

The norms you work with come into play as soon as you choose a category of performance you want to improve in a customer operation where you believe you can bring the contribution to profits closer to your normal performance. At that point, you compare the customer's current performance against your norms. If your norms are superior, you have a lead to prepare a Profit Improvement Proposal.

A matrix for warehousing your norms on an industry-specific basis is shown in Figure 1-1. For each line of business or business function that you sell to, enter the major operations within it that you affect across the horizontal axis and your major applications that can improve their performance down the vertical axis. Where each application intersects each operation, the matrix shows your normal range of added value. Your norms that rank as a customer industry's best practices identify the categories in which you can be the "category killer"—the owner of the standard value of its outcome. Killer norms are your brands, your "product line" of high-margin earners in return for their high added value.

Norms that are not best practices identify your commodity applications. They earn you less and cost you more to sell because you must compete against someone else's category killers.

When a customer operating manager calls out, "Who owns the norms for my performance in this category?" your voice must be the only one to answer if the question addresses one of your category-killer applications. If someone else answers, you may be redundant. If everyone else answers—which means that no one

Figure 1-1. Norm matrix.

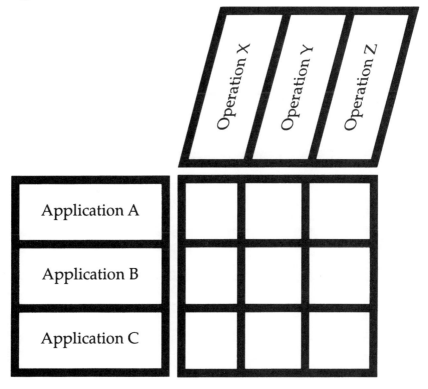

owns the norm—you are a vendor even if you call yourself a consultant.

A Norm-KPI Matrix modeled on the App-Op Matrix shown in Figure 1-1 can be used to provoke lead targeting by highlighting applications whose norms can improve key indicators of a customer's performance. This can make proposable PIP opportunities transparent and enable more fast closes.

In the form of digital dashboards, both matrices can be installed on a corporate intranet for real-time access on a 24/7 basis. They can be made customer-specific, so that only each customer's account manager can view them, or they can be open to an entire consultative sales force on a collaborative lottery basis: anyone who is first to suggest a winning value proposition receives a bonus that is percentaged on total PIP profits.

Digital dashboards can also be created to enable online assessment of consultative sellers' performance by their sales managers. An automated data collection process can help keep tabs on how each individual seller is performing according to key indicators as well as on team, industry, and regional performance. Key consultative seller performance indicators can include the ratio of PIPs closed to PIPs proposed, average cycle time to close, average investment-to-profit ratio per close, and average value of each migration PIP.

Making Norms Industry-Specific

Norms are meaningless unless they are industry-specific. Industry designations do not get specific until they are defined by a three-digit Standard Industrial Classification (SIC) code, such as the seven classes of Primary Metal Industries:

SIC Code	Industry Subcategory
331	Blast Furnaces and Basic Steel Products
332	Iron and Steel Foundries
333	Primary Nonferrous Metals
334	Secondary Nonferrous Metals
335	Nonferrous Rolling and Drawing
336	Nonferrous Foundries

Within each three-digit code are four-digit subclasses. The code 3321 contains gray and ductile iron foundries, while 3322 contains malleable iron foundries. As a general rule, three-digit norms suffice. But if you do a lot of business in a four-digit subclass, it will pay you to correlate your norms to its improved outcomes. Otherwise, a niche specialist can beat you.

Your norms must average the aggregate values you contribute to a specific operation in a line of business or business function in the industry as the result of each application.

Applications must be equally specific. The exact specifications, configurations, or installation requirements of an application may vary even within the same industry. Your norms should account for them by being prefaced with predictive modifiers, such as:

- Above/below average engineering changes
- Above/below average specification deviations
- Above/below average labor content
- Above/below average use of multiple materials
- Above/below average production of multiple parts
- Above/below average generation of multiple product variations that cause multiple customized setups
- Above/below average length of production runs

If you sell to manufacturing customers, you should create a correlate to the SIC classification system with an SPC Index for Standard Process Classifications and an SCC Index for Standard Cycle Classifications. You can model them like this:

Standard Workflow Classifications

001	Information Systems Workflow
002	R&D Workflow
003	Engineering/Product Development Workflow
004	Manufacturing Workflow
005	Inventory Workflow
006	Sales and Service Workflow

Standard Cycle Classifications

101	Product Design and Development Cycle
102	Production Cycle
103	Inventory Cycle
104	Order Entry/Shipment Cycle
105	Billing and Collection Cycle
106	Sales Cycle

A norm's worth is derived from its specific application-to-operation nature. This is the only way that your norms can act as shorthand representations of your ability to solve customer business problems: your norms for costs saved by reducing labor content or reducing scrap in a manufacturing operation, or your norms for revenues gained by speeding up product design and development cycle times in R&D.

Selling based on customer industry norms is commodity selling. Industry norms are commodities. They are available to you and to your competitors alike. They give you no meaningful differentiation. Nor do they give your customers the competitive advantage to take leadership even if you succeed in improving their current norms to the industry level. Industry norms are competitive floors, not ceilings. To perform at or near the industry norm is merely a customer's entry pass into competition, not a badge of superiority. Competitive parity is signaled by the industry norm. Competitive advantage takes place above it.

Bringing Customers Closer to Your Norms

As a norm leader, you can offer customers a demonstrable advantage over their competitors by bringing them closer to your norms, which should be significantly superior to the industry average. This ability—to help your customers compete more cost-effectively—is your own competitive advantage as a consultant. It transcends your product price and performance, your deals and discounts, features and benefits, or any other aspect of your business and its sales propositions. It is the added value that your customers buy when they buy from you.

Without norms, you cannot quantify prospective customers. You may be able to learn where they hurt; where their "pain points" are. But you cannot know how much you can ease the pain, if at all, or how long it may take. Nor can you know the value that easing the pain can add to the customers' operation where the hurt—or opportunity—is located.

If your customers are providers of supply chain management software and you supply solutions to businesses in the SIC code 7372, your experience tells you that they derive revenues primarily from software licenses and services such as consultation, maintenance, and training. You also know that their two major cost centers are R&D and sales, both of which account for about two-thirds of their total costs.

You are most likely to target your leads where the customers' major sources of revenue bunch up and where the major costs cluster. But without norms, you can end up asking of everything you learn, "So what?"

What if you learn that the customer's revenues from license fees have decreased 38 percent from a year ago? So what? If you do not have norms for the value you can add to license fee sales, how can you make a compelling proposal to increase them? By how much can you normally raise them? How soon? How sure can you be?

What if product development costs have been increasing by an average 23 percent year over year? So what? Can you help speed up the customers' innovation cycle time? Can you help expand the number of commercializable products that come out of their R&D? You cannot answer these questions unless you know how much value your solutions normally add and how soon they normally add it. Within the context of your norms, you can calculate your value propositions with maximum certainty that they can pay off.

If the customers' profits are coming more from turning over licenses at discounted fees instead of high unit margins, can you help? How sure are you? If their selling cycle takes an average of twelve months, can you reduce it? By how much? How soon? At what value to the customers? Based on the value, at what price to you?

The superior level of your norm value—superior to both the industry average and your customer's current performance in an operation's dollar contribution to profits—should brand you as the partner of choice. By contrast, your competitors who sell from industry norms will be selling commodities. Even though they can propose customer improvement, they cannot propose *leadership*.

Maintaining a superior norm margin is crucial to your branding. Every time you perform below it, you lower it; every time you lower it, you come back to the pack of competitive commodity suppliers. This is your main incentive to work at your best. It also warns you to work only with customers who want as badly as you do the growth that your norms promise, who have the managers and support staffs who can partner additively with you, and who will be impressive references for your track record as norm leader.

A model set of norms, in this case "norms on a card," is shown in Figure 1-2. The information on this three-by-five–inch card represents the normal savings that an automated process controls supplier can make in the major cost contributors to a pulp mill's operations.

Figure 1-2. Norms on a card.

Critical Success Factors	Norms for Cost Contrib/YR* ($000)
Labor	4,000
Chemicals	4,600
Wood	2,300
Energy	2,100
*250,000 Ton/YR Mill	

invested with them. What rate of return will be achieved? When will the investment be paid back? How abundantly will the cash flow? What is the degree of risk?

With every release of funds to a Box Two manager, a control procedure goes along with it to make sure that the invested funds are, first of all, paid back on time, and then maximized for the greatest return. The Box Two managers who get the most funds the most often are the best internal sellers. If you can help them get even more, or more often, they will "go partners" with you to do it again and again.

ALLYING BOX TWO

Consultative sellers succeed or fail on their ability to ally themselves with their Box Two counterparts. They cannot sell without them because Box Two *sells for them* in ways that they cannot. Their alliances are founded on creating an ongoing stream of Profit Improvement Proposals for the customer managers to sell internally, thereby obtaining the funds to support the consultative seller's strategies. In order to act consultatively, the seller must conform to the requirements outlined in Figure 2-1.

Box One thinks, feels, and acts in ways that are standard operating performance for all Box One managers, emulated by all Box Two managers who interface with them, and virtually unknown to everybody else. Box One's position self-description is that of a money manager.

As a money manager, Box One is preoccupied with financial stewardship, the management of other people's money. This involves making prudent, duly diligent investments, the control and fractionalizing of risk into small, survivable bites, and a conservative management style that emphasizes certainty over the chance for a windfall, incremental gains over breakthroughs, and consistency over flashes in the pan.

Your alliances at the Box Two level depend on the same standards of performance as your Box Two counterparts' internal alliance with their own Box One: the contributions that you make to competitive profit making. When you work in partnership with

2

HOW TO PENETRATE HIGH LEVELS

Top-tier customer management rarely deals with vendors, and then only under duress. They speak different languages. Vendors speak price and performance; management speaks value and profit. Vendors speak of their competitors; management is concerned about its own competition. Vendors wonder when management will ever buy; management wonders when vendors will ever leave.

Vendors who stand before their customer's top tier will not do so for long, or soon again. For consultative sellers to make a stand, and make it again and again, they must be prepared to speak the language of management, address customer concerns instead of their own, and put to work their knowledge of the customer's business so that a demonstrable improvement—not just a shipment of goods—takes place.

Key account sales representatives who want to penetrate the top customer tier must position themselves to discuss, document, and deliver their answers to the question, "How much profit will you add?"

In order to be accepted as profit improvers, sales representatives must pledge allegiance to the Consultant's Credo, reproduced in Figure 2-1. Only by understanding the consultant mindset—which is the mirror image of the customer manager mindset—will you be able to partner at the Box Two level shown in Figure 2-2. The customer business line managers and business function man-

Figure 2-1. Consultant's Credo.

Consultants sell money, not products. They transact returns from investments, not sales. Their price is an investment, not a cost. Their performance is measured by the amount and rate of the customer's return, not by product performance benefits. They work inside their customer businesses as partners, not from the outside as vendors. They relate directly to customer line-of-business managers and business function managers, not purchasing agents. They work at these middle management levels on a long-term, continuing basis, not from bid to bid. Their focus is not on competitive suppliers but on competitive profit making for their customer partners and for themselves.

agers are concentrated at this level, reporting directly to Box One, where the funds are.

Box One is the home of the "C Level" managers, the chief officers of operations, finance, information, and other core corporate functions, including the chief executive officer (CEO).

By partnering at Box Two, you can capture customer managers to act as your "economic sellers"—there is no such thing as "economic buyers," since Box Two managers do not buy—who will help you do your job so that you can help them do their jobs more successfully.

If you are a Box Two manager, what constitutes success? It means always improving your contribution to profits. For a business line manager, it means expanding revenues or increasing margins. For a business function manager, it means reducing costs. And where does the money come from to do these things? It comes from Box One. What is your role in this process? You must help your customer partners get more funds, and get them more quickly and more surely so that they can increase more revenues or margins and decrease more costs.

As Figure 2-2 shows, Box One is the keeper of the keys to the corporate treasury. Box One is Box Two's funder, open to sugges-

Figure 2-2. Customer-manager hierarchy.

tion twenty-four hours a day, seven days a week, from their Box Two managers on how corporate funds can be invested more cost-effectively—in other words, how to get "the biggest bang for the buck." Box Two managers are always in a proposal mode with their Box One funders, claiming a stake in the funding process for their own businesses or functions. Box One favors them on the basis of the strategic fit of their proposals with corporate growth policy and their adherence to financial objectives for each dollar

Box Two function managers, the added contribution you make to them becomes incremental to the contribution they have committed to make to Box One. That is why they will partner with you. The incremental value of your contribution becomes their test of how much you are worth as a partner.

The definition of *business partner* is therefore the customer manager's definition: someone who can add incremental value to the manager's contribution to profits. If you are going to qualify as a consultant partner, you must make yourself incrementally valuable to a business manager. This means you must deliver one or more of three types of added value:

1. You must enable your partners to *add more profits* than they would be able to contribute without you.
2. You must enable your partners to *add profits sooner* than they would be able to contribute without you.
3. You must enable your partners to *add profits with greater certainty* than they would be able to contribute without you.

These "deliverables" set the standards of performance for consultative sellers. You will be judged for your partnerability by the manager's answers to three questions: *How much* value do you propose to add? *How soon* do you propose to add it? *How sure* can I be that you will add as much value as you propose as soon as you propose to add it?

These are very different questions from the traditional ones raised at the Box Three purchasing interface. When vendors make their sales calls there, they are asked how much performance they can propose and how little price they can charge for it. But Box Two managers do not buy products; they invest in value. They do not buy at all; they sell proposals to obtain funds for their own operations. The Box One managers they sell to are your customers' ultimate buyers. They buy investment opportunities that can put their money to work at the highest rates for the surest return within the shortest periods of time.

They judge their Box Two operating managers by how good they are as money managers. "If I give you one dollar," they ask in effect, "How much more will you give me back? How long before I get it? How sure can I be?" Managers who partner with you as their consultative seller are betting that you can help them enhance their performance by enabling them to return more money than they could alone, or return it faster, and return it more surely.

When you reduce one of the Box Two managers' critical cost factors, you can help them improve the contribution they return from their operation. When you increase one of their critical revenue factors, you do the same. These are the mutual objectives of your cooperative partnerships because they are the achievements that improve your mutual profits.

Customer managers who meet the standards of performance for cooperative partnerability are called the *Alpha Managers,* the consultative sellers' comanagers on the customer side. The Alpha Managers are the owners of the contribution from a customer operation. The Alpha's name is signed in blood on the operation's business plan. He runs, supports, or supplies a line of business and is not to be confused with vendor selling's usual list of barnyard suspects like the political fox, the coaching goose, or the gatekeeper gander.

There is only one Alpha Manager per consultative seller per customer operation. This makes it crucial to partner the Alpha Manager; once lost to a competitor, the consultative seller is effectively denied penetration.

EMPOWERING BOX TWO WITH ADDED VALUE

Box Two managers have a simple set of needs:

1. They want money.
2. They want money now—yesterday would have been even better.
3. They want money so that they can make more money with it.

In order to position yourself for Consultative Selling, you must be able to prove to customer managers that you can help them get their hands on money, that you can help them to get it soon, and that you can supply them with a steady stream of investment opportunities that will enable them to make more money. These are the empowering features and benefits that will make you compellingly partnerable.

As your products and services become more closely replicated by competition, their features and benefits can no longer be differentiated enough to command a premium price. This places the burden of differentiation on you. Can you help customer managers make or save more money than your competitors can? Can you help them make or save it faster? Can you make them more certain by working with you? *Yes* answers are your sole competitive advantage because they provide the sole competitive advantage of your customer managers.

Vendors sell by asking purchasing managers at the Box Three level to let the sellers do their job: "Buy from me." Consultants sell by helping their Box Two partners do their own jobs better: "Win with me. If you put your money to work with me," the consultant's position says, "you will have more money back sooner and surer." At the same time, you will have a greater market share of a current market, or you will have gained entry into a new market, or you will have a reduced cost burden in an important operation or greater productivity. You will be competitively advantaged as either a market share leader or as the industry standard of value as the low-cost producer.

The Box Two connection is vital. It is the essential linkup that makes Consultative Selling work. Without it, vendors remain vendors at the Box Three level, as these comments—typical of trying to sell consultatively to an untrained and unpartnered purchasing function—show:

> "The customers have not responded. We try and try but at the end of our product demos, the same questions are still raised: what is the price and how much of a discount does it represent?"

> "We must be qualifying opportunities far too late in our customers' decision process. We have no time to PIP, just enough to propose a quote."

The true value of the competitive advantages you bring to customers is not in new profits themselves but in their investment value when they put them to work. How much more can they make on what they have just made with you? Funds always seek work. Idleness incurs opportunity cost. For this reason, you must have your next investment proposal in your hip pocket—actually, in your Account Penetration Plan—ready to present as soon as your current project has reached payback. This maintains your position squarely in the flow of funds while simultaneously repositioning your customers for the next round of being competitively advantaged by their partnership with you.

As your customer partners position you, you are an optional investment opportunity. This is how you must come across to them. It tells you how you must define the nature of your business with them:

- If you are in the telecommunications business, you must not simply be "in telecom." You must not sell switches, networks, or rates.
- You must not be simply one more "problem solver." You must not just sell "solutions."
- You must not simply be a "consultant."

You must be a *profit improver*, a partner whose expertise and experience in the customers' businesses can help the customers increase the amount, speed, and certainty of the profits they contribute to their top-tier managers in Box One. You must understand the world that your partner lives in. If they are "in manufacturing" and considering robotics, they live in a world of cost contributors, such as Figure 2-3 shows. Which of them can you help the customers control? Your contributions are your tickets of entry into their world. How much you can contribute, how soon, and how reliably will determine whether you will be invited to live in your customers' world as their partner or will just be passing through.

POSITIONING AS THE MIXMASTER

Each customer business function is a mix of costs and opportunities. Can you optimize the customer's mix—that is, can you

50

Figure 2-3. Robotics cost checklist.

Acquisition Costs

- The robot and its tooling
- Facilities, equipment revisions, and rearrangements
- Application engineering
- Process and product changes
- Training and transfers
- Installation
- Direct labor costs

Life Cycle Costs
(Costs of Ownership)

- Cost of capital
- Taxes and insurance
- Maintenance labor, supplies, and spare parts
- Energy
- Training
- Scrap and rework
- Safety and potential cost of disability

enable it to more nearly deliver its optimal contribution to profits? If you can learn how to master the mix of customer costs in an industry's manufacturing process, for example, you can ensure your role as the industry's standard-bearer.

All customers allocate certain resources to each of their businesses and their functions. This is their asset base—actually, their cost base. Some of these resources are supplied internally. They consist of their own people and the capital they use. The rest of their resources come from outside—the products, services, and systems that are acquired from a variety of suppliers. Taken together, these internal and external resources form the customers' current operating "mix." In order to partner, you will have to help create a mix that can contribute higher profits.

All customer businesses operate with a mix. Some mixes are simply conglomerations of products. Others add services such as training or maintenance. Still others are composed of systems that, in turn, are composed of subsystems or, when amalgamated, contribute to networks. You must determine where you fit in every mix, what value you can add to it, and what the worth of that value can be to you and a customer.

The mix becomes your market. It is where you fit, where you operate, where you belong. It becomes the arena of your expertise. You must know how to make it produce profits in the most cost-effective manner, and you must know this better than anyone else. You must master the mix so well that you can position yourself with customers as their industry's "mixmaster."

Customer mixes usually lag behind the optimal mix. They frequently represent a sizable investment. They are also hidebound to a customer's learning curve. People have learned how to operate the current mix and have become familiar with its capabilities and its quirks. Training programs have been built around it. Cost and production schedules are established for it. Psychologically, it has become "the way we do things around here," a part of the gruel of corporate culture. It must be approached remedially but respectfully. You must not want to run your customers' businesses. You must want to partner with them so that *they can run them better.*

There are three main strategies for optimizing a customer's operating mix:

1. You can supplant one or more elements in the current mix. If the mix is labor-intensive, for example, you may be able to reduce labor content by substituting an automated process or eliminating an operation altogether. Or you may be able to combine multiple processes such as forecasting and inventory control, thereby eliminating overlapping and duplicated costs.

2. You can substitute your product or process for a competitive product or process that is part of the customer's current mix. The basis for your recommendation must be that improved financial benefits will accrue to the customer if the mix is altered—not simply that more advantageous performance benefits will be realized.

3. You can manage the mix internally as its systems integrator or facilities manager, working under a profit-improvement

contract with a customer. Alternatively, you can manage the mix as its outsourcer.

The specific strategies for partnering by means of optimizing a customer's mix depends on the industry you serve. If you sell personal care products to supermarket and drug chains, you can penetrate by optimizing the mix of the number of facings that stores allocate to your products compared to competitors', the locations of your facings, and the type of displays. The proof of your optimization has to be quantified in financial benefits, such as profit improvement per square foot, overall improvement from personal care department contribution per store, or improved profit contribution from related item sales. Or you may propose to optimize a customer's mix by taking on the role of manager of the personal care product category.

If you sell financial services such as stocks and bonds, insurance, real estate investments, or money market funds to affluent individuals, you can optimize the mix of their portfolios in terms of growth potential, risk, and current payout. The proof of your optimization has to be quantified in dollar benefits, such as higher earnings, lowered taxes, or increased net worth.

Customers are preoccupied with growth. In business, you grow or die. Without growth, costs overtake you, new technologies outmode you, and competitors outmarket or outflank you. Customer managers take partners precisely to hedge against these risks.

All consultants discover that it is easier to reduce a customer's costs than to expand sales, and it is a good deal easier to quantify the resulting improvement to profits from cost reductions. But consultants quickly learn that no customer business exists to control costs. Customers are in business to make money, and the only way to make money is through sales. A consultant who is positioned as a cost reducer can be important to a customer. But a consultant who is positioned as a sales developer is vital.

New profits from increasing customers' volume at the same margin or increasing margins at the same volume are the stuff of which growth is made. As a result, customers can control more of a market and become the profit leader if not the leader in market share. There is nothing wrong with being low-cost producers. But if consultants are expert in cost reduction, they should learn how to translate their impact into its effect on revenues so that they can be positioned as growth contributors.

All cost reductions can be translated into their sales equivalent. A reduction in the cost contributed by unnecessary inventory expense can be interpreted as the equivalent of a corresponding increase in sales revenues. This is equally true for a decrease in the cost contributed by scrap from off-specification production, from rejects or rework, from failures to make same-day delivery, from late billing, and from late collection of accounts receivable. If these costs are reduced, their earnings equivalent is the dollars saved or avoided: How much profit on how many dollars' worth of how many units sold over how much time stated as "the equivalent in profits from the sale of 500,000 cartons each week—or 1,000 carloads every seventy-two hours—or ten additional aircraft operating each day at an 80 percent load factor."

COMPETING AGAINST A CUSTOMER'S COMPETITION

Vendors compete against each other. Their customers pay their Box Three managers to manage this competition, playing one vendor off against another to get the best—that is, the lowest—price. Competition, whether among vendors or others, is based on comparison. When vendors compete for Box Three, they compare themselves against their competition product by product, feature and benefit by feature and benefit. When all the distinctions without a difference cancel out, vendors compare their performance to their price. In this way, they force debate on the relative merits—or, in other words, they force competition on themselves. The winners make the sale but, in the process, trade away their margins.

It is not uncommon for the margin loss to exceed 50 percent. In one typical case, a sales representative "sold" a $3 million order for computers to a retailer at a 54.75 percent discount that, the customer was told, would "elevate your awareness of the benefit of doing business with us by increasing your overall profitability." The discount was composed of a 46 percent price break plus free cooperative advertising funds, prepaid freight, the services of a team of marketing and sales representatives, together with a product trainer, and a rebate program. As the representative said who made the sale, "The customer practically sold himself."

The transcendent objective of Consultative Selling is to maintain premium margins. To do this, consultants must create a new concept of competition; that is, they must sponsor a different set of comparisons, none of which is with "other vendors." In addressing Box Two, consultants can position two types of comparison for their customers to evaluate:

1. For profit center managers who run customer business lines, consultants can create a comparison between a manager's current sales and share of market and the consultant's norms. When the consultants' norms are superior, they can propose to add value to the customer by helping to increase volume or margins.
2. For cost center managers who run customer business functions, consultants can create a comparison between a manager's current operating performance and the consultant's norms. When the consultants' norms are superior, they can propose to add value to the customer by helping to reduce or avoid costs.

In both cases, the consultative sellers are challenging the customer to compare their current competitive advantage with a proposed superior advantage. Is a competitor taking greater advantage of a market opportunity than you are? If so, I can help you come closer to equality or leadership. Are unnecessarily costly operations taking needless advantage of your profits and preventing you from being a lower cost producer? If so, I can help you come closer to equality or leadership.

When customers focus on comparing what it is costing them now, in both direct costs and opportunity costs, to be competitive with what it could cost them if they were partnered with the consultant, their concentration is on their own competitive position and not the consultant's. Other vendors are driven from their field of vision. They are out of sight and out of mind because the questions the customers ask themselves have nothing to do with "the best price." They are, instead, preoccupied with questioning the deal at hand. Is it credible—can I believe the numbers? Is it sufficient—will it make enough of a difference? Can it be done—can the proposed people and systems and strategies do the job? Is it realistic—can I reasonably expect to get the predicted rate of return on my investment within the promised time frame?

What if they ask, "Are there other suppliers who could do the same thing or do it more cheaply or better or faster?" They already know the answer: "Perhaps." They also know that because time is money, they will risk opportunity cost if they want to find out. They will be far more concerned with evaluating today's opportunity today—the bird in the hand—and not speculating about tomorrow. All they can ever be sure about is today. Today's opportunity taken tomorrow is already operating at a competitive disadvantage.

ZEROING IN ON CONSULTATIVE TARGETS

In order to be able to improve the profit contribution of a customer's business or business function, you must know three things:

1. The current values in the customer business or function that you can affect—the dollar values of a customer's current costs, current productivity levels, and current sales
2. The prospective dollar values that you can add
3. The net worth of your added dollar values when subtracted from the investment required to realize them

Knowing Customer Current Values

All customer operations are cost centers. Only one, the sales function, can also be a profit center if profits from sales exceed the cost of sales. Customers have a choice of three strategies for managing their operations. One is to avoid or reduce costs while maintaining productivity. Another is to increase productivity while maintaining, reducing, or even increasing costs. The third is to eliminate an operation altogether, either spinning it out as an independent profit center to remove it from the corporate books or outsourcing it.

- In order to consult with a *customer line-of-business manager (LOB),* you must be expert in the customer's markets. This means that you must have three kinds of smarts. You must be *process smart,* knowledgeable in the flow of the customer's products through their distribution processes and where their critical values are added. You must be *applications smart,* knowledgeable in how to apply your products and services to the customer's sales and distribution process so that revenues or margins can be increased. And you must be *validation smart,* knowledgeable in how to quantify your contribution.

"Knowing your customer's business" means having all three types of smarts. In the areas of your expertise, you must know how a customer's distribution process flows. You must be able to chart it from start to finish. You must know the 20 percent of its critical success factors that contribute up to 80 percent of its income and earnings. You must know the value of these revenues and profits. You must know your norms for the products and markets that account for the majority of profits and by how much the customer's earnings deviate from them. You must know how to bring the customer's profits closer to a norm if they are below it or keep them above it if the customer is doing better than the norm. You must know by how much you can do this and how soon. When you know all these things, then you can say that you know the customer's business as far as the products and markets you affect are concerned. Anything less is vendor selling.

- In order to consult with a *customer function manager,* who supports or supplies a line of business, you must be expert in his or her operation. This means that you must have three kinds of smarts. You must be *process smart,* knowledgeable in the flow of the customer's process and where the critical costs cluster. You must be *applications smart,* knowledgeable in how to apply your products and services to the customer's process so that costs can be reduced or productivity can be increased. And you must be *validation smart,* knowledgeable in how to quantify your contribution.

"Knowing your customer's business" means having all three types of smarts. In the areas of your expertise, you must know how a customer's process flows. You must be able to chart it from start to finish. You must know the 20 percent of its critical success factors that contribute up to 80 percent of its costs. You must know the value of these costs. You must know your norms for these operations and by how much the customer's costs deviate from them. You must know how to bring the customer's costs closer to a norm if they exceed it or keep them below it if the customer is doing better than the norm. You must know by how much you can do this and how soon. When you know all this, you can say you know the customer's business as far as the operations you affect are concerned. Anything less is vendor selling.

Vendors like to say that they are value adders. Yet all they can usually quantify is the value of the cost they add when a customer buys from them. Rarely, if ever, do they know the value of the customer costs they reduce or the productivity they increase or the new revenues and profits they contribute to. Yet these are every supplier's most crucial values. Unless you know them, you are selling blind. You will only be as valuable as your most recent discount.

Even worse, you are selling costs, not improved profits, when you vend. If you do not know the value you add to a customer, you must sell what you know: your product's cost and its justification. As soon as you sell cost, you will come under the control of the customer's purchasing function, whose primary purpose is cost control. You will be imprisoned in vending.

Arranging a Transfer of Values

In Consultative Selling terms, a *sale* is a transfer of values: A customer's resources—time, talent, and money—are transferred for the contribution to customer profits made by a supplier's products and services. In the same terms, a *sales call* must be an exchange of values as well. The customers must come away with new knowledge: They must be aware of the supplier's norms for profit contribution and how the current contributions of their operations compare with them. The suppliers must come away with new knowledge as well, consisting of data on customer businesses or business functions whose profit contributions can be brought closer to the suppliers' norms—in other words, they must come away with *leads*. Unless the suppliers come home with data on which to base a Profit Improvement Proposal, or with an approved proposal itself, they have not made a sales call. They have been socializing on company time.

All value is customer value. Adding value does not take place at the factory. It takes place in a customer's business. If you are going to add to a customer's value, you must first know what it is without your addition. This is the customer's "before." The new value will be the customer's "after." The difference between before and after is the *value added by your business*. In truth, it *is* your business. It is what you do and the reason why you are in business to do it.

For the purposes of Consultative Selling, the value you add must become the product you sell. You must become a value-added seller. This means that you must know your "product," the value that you represent.

In common with all products, value has its own specifications. These give it its performance capability, that is, what it is able to do inside a customer's business. Your performance capability is customer-dependent and will vary for each customer application. Each of your "products" will be unique to its customer. No two values will be the same, except by chance. As a result, you will no longer be able to print a price list. As values differ customer by customer, moving up and down within the range that establishes your norms, the price you require in the form of a customer's investment to achieve each value will also differ.

Value has three specifications:

1. *It has "muchness"*: You will be able to add a lot of value or only a little.
2. *It has "soonness"*: You will be able to add value quickly or not for a while.
3. *It has "sureness"*: You will be able to add value with a high degree of certainty or you will hedge.

A mix of "muchness," "soonness," and "sureness" forms the value benefits that you will be able to offer to each customer. You must be able to quantify each one. Otherwise, if all you can say is something like, "We are pretty sure that we can provide a lot of value to your operation very soon," you will be saying nothing. Once you have quantified your value, then you will be able to know your most important sales tool: what your added value is worth to your customers.

Knowing the Worth of Your Added Values

If you are able to offer your customers the added value of one dollar as the result of doing business with you, what are you really offering them? The dollar has three values. One is its money value. A dollar is a dollar. Another value is its time value. A dollar today is worth more than the same dollar will be worth tomorrow. Finally, the dollar has investment value. It can be invested at a rate of return that will multiply its original value several times.

Your value is worth what customers can do with it—a function of how much they get from you, when they get it, and what they do with it. This is the ultimate worth of your dollar. Like value, dollars appreciate only inside the customers' business. In order to create new worth for customers, you must therefore get into the customers' business—into their critical lines of business and critical business functions—and help them manage them. You cannot create worth without the customers. Nor can they achieve the added worth you offer without you. To magnify the worth of a business, you and your customers need each other. This congruence of need makes you partnerable.

As a consultant, the most important knowledge you can have about your business is *your value* to your customers; that is, how much you typically contribute to their profits and how long it typically requires to make your contribution.

When you know what your value is worth to customers, you and your customers can tell what kind of consultant material you represent. If your value is the same as what the customers can obtain working alone without you, you are not consultant material. If your value is worth more than what the customers can obtain working alone or with any other supplier, you may be prime consultant material.

If you want to be the customers' consultant, you must offer them the prime value. Nobody must be able to offer better value specifications—as much value or as soon or as sure. If you can achieve this position, your value becomes the industry standard. Not only do you deliver the greatest value, but it is worth the most to your customers.

When that happens, you have a new basis for your price. No longer does your price need to reflect cost or competitive market value. You are able to relate your price to the worth of your value on a return-on-investment basis. The customers' added worth becomes their return. Your price becomes their investment. A premium return to the customers is all the justification you need to require a premium investment.

If you sell without knowing your value, everything else you know is rendered valueless for margin building. What price would you charge—or, in Consultative Selling terms, what investment would you require—for sixty two-way wireless radios installed on the manufacturing floor of an engine maker's plant? If you guess $150,000 because you do not know that the customer's first-year cost savings from reduced downtime is $1.5 million, what kind of a deal would you have made if you had given your product away while its value-to-price ratio was 10 to 1? You would have booked the sale, but you would have made yourself a philanthropist.

3

HOW TO MERIT
HIGH MARGINS

For both consultative sellers and their customers, profit is the name of the game. While the game is the same, the role you play in it is very different from that of your customer.

Setting profit objectives is the customer's business. It cannot be abdicated, nor can the customer delegate it to anyone outside the company. No one who is external to a company can ever know enough about total corporate assets and liabilities—financial, operational, or human—to set business objectives based on them. Besides, your concern with a customer's business is rarely with all of it. Your concern is concentrated on the application or use of the product and service systems with which you yourself are involved. As a result, your role is concerned with the additive effects that the value of your product and service systems can have on the customer's profitability. You are each customer's *incremental profit improver*, not total profit maker.

A customer's primary management function is to develop strategic and tactical plans that can achieve profit maximization. Your role is limited to profit betterment. This means that you will propose your contribution from the point at which customers have finished developing their own profit plans. The end point of the customer's profit objectives becomes your point of departure.

Every value that a PIP adds to a customer is incremental to the customer's current values. This means that the overhead of fixed costs already being funded by the customer can be made to contribute additional values without adding to it. PIPs require no additional plants to be built, no new R&D facilities to be developed, and no new customer sales managers or representatives to be hired. PIPs make the customer's current overhead more productive and less costly, leveraging small investments into significantly higher returns.

This is why consultative sellers propose in terms of "contribution." It is not their own ability to contribute profits they are proposing. Instead, they are being consultative in helping their customers produce a greater contribution from current assets.

VALUE-BASING CUSTOMER INVESTMENT

Whatever a price is attached to is called the *product*. It is the thing sold; it is what the customer is asked to pay for. Vendors affix a price tag to hardware or software or a system that combines both of them. Consultative sellers eliminate the concept of price, replacing it with an investment to apply products, services, or systems at a profit to their customers. In this way, the investment is repaid by the value that comes out of it. The cost to the customer—the price—is zero.

Once price is eliminated, cost vanishes. So does fair market value set by competitive prices as a pricing standard. Value to the customers becomes the basis point for their investment, a way of doing business that Becton Dickinson has discovered about its hypodermic needles sold to hospitals. When purchasing agents were the customers, they complained that 10 cents was too much to pay for needles that they bought from competitors for 7 cents. Becton's vendor reflex was to wage a profitless price war. But a value analysis showed that accidental needlesticks cost a hospital an average $400 each in time and paperwork charges even if there were no complications or legal expenses.

What if Becton could reduce the costs contributed by needlesticks by more than the 3 cents difference in the price of needles offered by a competitor? What is Becton's value to the customer? What is a fair investment for a customer to make to acquire it— fair in proportion to the value of the return, not to the price of the hypodermic needles? Should Becton sell needles on price or on the value of needlestick prevention derived from advanced needle technology, training programs for hospital staff, and consultative expertise in safety program implementation?

Hewlett-Packard made a similar discovery. In the same quarter that its earnings fell 46 percent because "pressure on gross margins prevented revenue growth from being translated into earnings"—in other words, price competition was eating up margins—an analysis of H-P's added value showed how much margin potential H-P was leaving on the table by vending its computer systems on price and performance:

- For one customer, each $100,000 paid to H-P contributed $1.2 million in reduced costs, for a value-to-price ratio of 12:1.
- For another customer, each $250,000 paid to H-P contributed $8.75 million in new revenues, for a value-to-price ratio of 35:1.

The alternative to knowing your value and selling it is discounting your price. Once you give away your margin to make a sale, you never get it back. Discounting is relentless in the way it destroys profits:

- If you start out with a 50 percent margin and you discount it by 10 percent, you must sell 25 percent more product in order to realize the same revenues.
- If you start out with a 35 percent margin, you must sell 40 percent more.
- If you start out with a 20 percent margin, you must sell 100 percent more.

Another way to look at it is if a product's costs remain steady at 91.9 percent of its $1.00 sales price, a 3 percent discount reduces profit from 8.1 percent to 5.1 percent—a 37 percent loss on the new price of 97 cents.

It is a myth that you can "make it up on volume." The cost of sales goes up with volume, nullifying increases in revenues. If a 3 percent discount produces an average 5 to 6 percent increase in volume, for example, it takes four cycles of 3 percent discounts to get a 20 percent increase in volume when unit costs first begin to fall. In other words, sales must increase by one-fifth just to get back to where you started.

Companies that do not understand price-value relationships go out of business. When Digital Equipment began to fall from its number two position in the computer industry, founder Ken Olsen thought he saw the reason. "We were selling computers while the customers wanted solutions to business problems," he said. "You can see at DECWorld that we've addressed that." But press service reports of DECWorld described it as "a showcase of the company's innovative technology and product line."

Even innovative technology cannot help to maintain margin when the technology itself and not its problem-solving value is sold. Digital's Alpha AXP microprocessor was the fastest high-performance computer chip of its time. Yet Digital was forced to successively discount its price by as much as 31 percent per cut over several rounds of cuts. All the while, the Alpha AXP remained the world's fastest chip and its manufacturer remained the most ignorant about its value.

Assessing value before assigning price, and then basing price on value, is bedrock Consultative Selling strategy. Otherwise, money—often sums that are even greater than the volume of sales that are made—will surely be left on the table.

David Liddle, CEO of Metaphor Computer Systems, made this discovery after retroactively calculating the value added to nine major customers where Metaphor systems had been in place for two to three years. He found that the average revenue gain in just the 12 prior months was $8.7 million that could be directly attributed to Metaphor. For the next three years, the same customers were projecting an even greater average 15:1 annual return on their systems. Liddle's reaction was to kick himself for having sold to all nine customers at 30 percent to 40 percent discounts from his $1.25 million price.

If Liddle had known his value beforehand and simply maintained his price, his customers would have realized more than $8 for every $1 they paid him. Instead of discounting, he could have reclaimed even more of his value at an even higher price.

If you are not prepared to improve a customer's profits, the customer will always be prepared to reduce your own profits. After one year of operation of a Xerox Advanced Document System, Continental Insurance of Canada was approached by a Xerox competitor who offered to buy out the Document System from Continental and replace it with its own system at half the Xerox price. In order to keep the business, Xerox met the offer at a loss of over $500 thousand.

After doing the deal, Xerox went into Continental's operations to learn what it should have known all along: in 12 months, Continental's use of the Advanced Document System had added $17.7 million in incremental revenues at a net operating margin of $1.9 million. Yet without knowing its value, Xerox was required to compete on price.

A customer's improved profitability should immunize his supplier against having to discount price. A manufacturing customer who is able to apply a supplier's product to decrease his R&D's contribution to a new product's development cost by $1.60 million has no justification for discounting a $1.00 million price. But when the savings come from reducing the innovation cycle by 6 months so that incremental revenues of $1.5 million accrue in year one that would have otherwise been zero, it is the supplier who is justified in value-basing price.

The only way to avoid discounts is to sell your added value and not your product or service. In the same way that you cannot make it up on volume, you cannot get around it by other, less visible price offers such as sweetened payment terms, additional warranty coverage, or free training giveaways that are simply discounts in disguise.

GENERATING PROFIT IMPROVEMENT PROPOSALS

A consultative seller's day-to-day work is the generation of Profit Improvement Proposals. Each PIP adds value to your customer's profit objectives through the application of your product and service systems to the customer's business operations.

66

Through such added value, you are able to merit added margins in return.

The process of generating profit proposals must be a continuing one. Once it begins, it can go on endlessly because the profit-improvement opportunities in a customer company are limitless.

You will find the task of selecting your profit-improvement portfolio easier if you apply five criteria. They will steer you toward PIPs that have the greatest chance of succeeding.

1. *New profits should be achievable within 365 days.* Longer time frames incur unpredictable risks. They not only defy ready calculation but invite disenchantment or cancellation of PIP projects already under way.

2. *New profits should be significant for both you and your customer.* Shared profit improvement should not be confused with equal profit. The first objective—profitability for both—is a vital aspect of the concept of partnership. The second—equal profit—is both impossible and unnecessary.

3. *New profits must draw on a major product or service capability* to be profitable for your company. Similarly, in order for your customer to profit, your proposals must affect a major product, service, or operation.

4. *New profits must be measurable* in terms of a net increment or a decremental investment in operating assets. If it cannot be measured, or if no provision is made to quantify it, agreement on whether improvement even took place may be impossible to obtain.

5. *New profits should not be an isolated entity* but a module that leads naturally to the next infusion of profits and then to the next one after that.

Box Two business managers are managers of cost centers or profit centers. Whatever operation their particular business function may perform or whatever markets their line of business may sell to, they are essentially in the business of asset management. They are funded by their Box One managers with assets in the form of cash or credit. They are expected to invest these assets in their operations to turn a profit on the original investment, which they will allocate to fixed and operating assets "under management." How good they are at this determines how much they will get the next time.

Consultative sellers can take on the role of contributing to their Box Two partner's success as an asset manager in three ways:

1. They can help their customer managers improve their ratio of selling successful proposals to Box One by adding high-quality investment opportunities to the managers' portfolio and helping them to obtain more funds.
2. They can help their customer managers improve their turnover rate of accepted proposals to Box One by adding more investment opportunities to the managers' portfolio and helping them turn them over faster.
3. They can help their customer managers improve their success ratio of implementing projects by adding expertise that will help earn more profits or earn them sooner and with greater certainty.

Consultative Selling is based on a universal management principle: Never add an asset to a customer operation without an asset management program to reduce its cost of ownership or to earn back more than its price.

For customer businesses in many industries, infinitesimally small problems can add up to significant costs. A leak of only 0.01 percent of oil passing through a refinery valve can add up to 1.2 barrels per hour, 28.8 barrels per day, and 10,512 barrels per year. At $10 a barrel, one leaking valve can cost $105,120 in lost annual sales.

If you sell leakproof valves, the $105,120 revenue gain per valve—multiplied by the total number of leaking valves in the refinery—is your product.

In a similar way, a $75,600 revenue gain per valve is your product if you can stop contamination from leaking into a 2,520 million gallon premium oil tank and downgrading it to regular oil that must be sold for $.03 less per gallon.

In business, money has one purpose: to make more money.

To be a consultative seller, you must position yourself as adding the values of "more money faster and surer" to your customers. This is the supreme product. All customers need it all the time. There is always demand—no matter what you sell—because no matter how much money is on hand, there is always a short supply. There is never enough soon enough; "more money yesterday" is the only answer a Box Two manager ever gives to the question, "How much do you want and when do you want it?"

Every dollar that Box Two managers have is on loan to them. The loan, in the form of allocated funds from Box One, is callable on the date that the managers' proposals have pledged to achieve payback on Box One manager's investments. But that is only the beginning. Box One managers do not invest to achieve payback. Their objective is to maximize the return on their investment and to do so as quickly as possible. In this sense, the funds they lend to the Box Two managers who report to them are trust funds: Box One managers trust their Box Two managers to return the funds at a profit.

POSITIONING PROFIT IMPROVEMENT

Positioning an improvement in customer profits is a three-step process: (1) definition of a customer problem to be solved or a customer opportunity to be capitalized; (2) prescription of the profit-improvement benefit from solving the problem or capitalizing on the opportunity; (3) and description of the operational and financial workings of the system that can yield the improved profit.

Step 1: Problem/Opportunity Definition

Your initial task is to establish consultant credibility. Initial credibility comes only from displaying knowledge of a customer's business. Until a customer can say, "That supplier knows my business," the customer will rarely be inclined to say, "That supplier can improve my profit."

In fact, you must be knowledgeable about two areas of a customer's business. First, you must know the location of significant cost centers that are susceptible to reduction. Second, you must know how a customer's customers can be induced to buy more from the customer. In the first instance, you must prescribe a system that will reduce customer costs. This is a problem-solving system. In the second instance, you must prescribe a system that will increase customer sales. This is an opportunity-seizing system.

Defining a customer problem or opportunity has two parts: what you know and how you know it. The second part documents the first by citing the sources of your knowledge. It also reinforces your credibility. There are three likely sources of knowledge about a customer cost problem or sales opportunity. One is that the customer revealed it. This is the "horse's mouth" source. A second source of knowledge is past experience with the customer, with other companies in the same industry, or your track record symbolized by its norms. The third is that knowledge can come from homework. This is the "midnight oil" source.

Step 2: Profit-Improvement Prescription

The objective of the first step in a consultative presentation is to say to a customer, in effect: "You have a situation that is detrimental to your profit. Either you are incurring unnecessary costs or you are failing to capture available sales revenues." The objective of the second step is to say, "Working together, we can reduce some of those costs or gain some of those sales as a cost-beneficial investment."

In this way, you further reinforce the perception of being knowledgeable about the customer's business by framing the system's benefit in businesslike terms of return on investment. By quantifying an added value the system can make to the customer's operations, you are creating a business-manager-to-business-manager context for customer decision making in contrast to a vendor-to-purchaser context.

The prescription for customer profit improvement must specify the positive return that can predictably result from installation of your system. The return should be specified as both a percentage rate of improvement and its equivalent in dollars. These quantifications, the end-benefit specifications in money terms, rather than specifics about the system's performance or components, are the ultimate specifications of the consultant's system. These are what a customer will or will not buy. They are therefore what you must prescribe for delivery.

IBM consultants approach top-tier management of key retail customers on behalf of IBM's computer-assisted checkout station. The consultants prescribe profit improvement benefits of reduced costs and increased sales like this: "For a store with gross weekly sales of $140,000, savings are projected at $7,650 a month by faster customer checkout and faster balancing of cash registers." The time required to check out an average order is said to be reduced by almost 30 percent. In addition, IBM sales representatives claim that the elimination of time and cost expenses of correcting checker errors can contribute annual savings of more than $91,000 per store.

If a store is growing, its total savings every year can approach one week's gross sales at the $140,000 level. The net value of these savings falls directly to the store's bottom line. The essential contribution made by IBM is providing added growth funds that supplement revenues from sales and can be invested for still further growth. In the course of making its contribution, IBM consultatively sells computers.

The same solution can often make a contribution to decreasing customers' costs as well as increasing their revenues. In almost every case, the increased revenues exceed the cost savings. Revenues are also the reason customers are in business. So it is always preferable to sell the revenue gain rather than the cost reduction, unless the costs being reduced are costs of sale. In that event, a profit-centered line-of-business manager will be responsible for both.

The preeminence of revenues over cost savings does not mean you should not sell profit improvement through cost reduction. It means that you have two options, one of which is generally to be preferred.

If you sell simulation software that lets a manufacturing customer design new products on computer screens instead of by constructing physical prototypes, you can affect customer revenues and costs at the same time:

• You can affect revenues by helping the customer get new products to market faster, create products that are more reliable, longer lasting, and more energy-efficient, that are safer, that have better styling, and that are easier to customize.

• You can affect costs by reducing the number of physical models and tests, using fewer engineers and less design time, using less material, reducing repair costs under warranty and cutting down on recalls, paying for fewer design changes, lowering training costs, and reducing nonperformance penalties and late charges.

How do you decide which to sell?

Your decision must be based on comparative contribution:

What are the revenue gains from helping the customers get faster to market with a new model? How long do they take to pay back the investment and pay out the proposed improved profits?

How do the revenue gains compare to the costs saved by increased design productivity, with its labor and time savings?

How do the savings from design productivity plus savings from reduced warranty costs compare to the revenue gains in their muchness and soonness?

Does any combination of cost savings compare favorably with the proposed revenue gains?

In spite of the fact that cost reductions are typically less than revenue expansions, they can have five saving graces. First, costs are easier to quantify. Second, costs can often be reduced faster than revenues can accrue.

Because costs are internal, a third advantage can be the greater certainty of realizing a proposed saving than an added revenue stream. Fourth, once a cost is reduced or eliminated, it stays removed forever and can be credited year after year, indefinitely. And fifth, cost savings may be the most cost-effective strategy for mature customers in oligarchic markets where market shares can only be traded, not gained.

Step 3: System Specification

The third presentation step is to specify the system that will deliver the promised profit-improvement mix and to justify its premium price by interpreting price in terms of investment in the new mix. Customers must not be asked to buy systems; you must invite them to improve profit. They are not quoted a system's price; you must promise them a positive return on the investment in their system.

The purpose of defining the system is not to sell it, but rather to present proof that the promised benefit is derived from known capabilities that have been prescribed precisely because they will contribute in the most cost-beneficial way to the customer's profit improvement. The system substantiates your promise. Its capabilities, plus your personal expertise in applying them, are the means of conferring new profitability on the customer.

Defining a customer problem or opportunity should condition a customer to relate to you as a business manager. The next presentation step, prescribing a quantified benefit, should condition a customer to regard the system as a profit-making investment, not as a cost or a collection of components. Defining the system and justifying its price should condition a customer to credit the prescription as believable and achievable.

The final step in a system's presentation is to set down the standards by which you progressively monitor the system's ability to deliver the promised benefit in partnership with the customer. At least three control standards should be set so that a working partnership can be confirmed between consultant and customer:

1. Time frames for the accomplishment of each installation and operational stage
2. Checkpoints for measuring the impacts of phasing the system into customer business functions
3. Periodic progress review and report sessions to head off problems and anticipate new applications and opportunities for system extension, upgrading, modernization, and replacement

The comparative analysis of customers' costs to improve their profits by doing business with you and the benefits they can expect to receive are the heart of Consultative Selling. Cost-benefit analysis, which should really be called "investment-return analysis," positions profit projects as fundable or scrap. It tells customers how much they must lay out for how much they can get back. The basic format for costing the benefits of a profit improvement project with a five-year commercial life is shown in Figure 3-1. Compare it with Figure 9-1, which shows a similar analysis of an investment's costs and benefits in the software format of PIPWARE.

Figure 3-2 is a glossary of guidelines to analyze the relationship between costs and the benefits that flow from them.

POSITIONING PROFIT PROJECTS

A PIP is a profit project. Its site is customers' premises, either one of their business lines or a business function. A PIP is a money-making project. It says to the customers, "Here is where you are incurring unnecessary costs or missing out on realizable revenues. Here is what it is costing you. Here is how much you can save or earn. Here is what it will take to obtain the improvement and how long it will be before you can see it on your bottom line."

PIPs are designed to affect customers' economies. To do this, they require adding the value of a supplier's products or services along with information in the form of advisory services and training. Sometimes financing is involved as time payments or a lease. But the essential ingredient in every project is its manager.

Positioning a profit-improvement project is a consultative seller's prime skill. This requires sellers to be good diagnosticians, making sure they have sized up the project correctly from the outset. The sellers must then be good prescribers in order to propose the most cost-effective solution for the problem or opportunity they have diagnosed. Then they must be good installers, implementers, and appliers to fit the solution seamlessly into customers' operations so that it becomes a part of their natural flow. They must be good planners, exactly meeting each milestone along the way from startup through payback to realization of the proposal's objective. And at every step of the way, they must be good partners with their customers' people, without whose cooperation they can accomplish nothing.

Customers who are being PIPped must perceive that they are

(Text continues on p. 77)

Figure 3-1. Cost-benefit work flow.

Investment	Y0	Y1	Y2	Y3	Y4	Y5
Cash Out						

Contribution from Increased Sales	Y1	Y2	Y3	Y4	Y5
Cash In					

Contribution from Reduced Costs	Y1	Y2	Y3	Y4	Y5
Cash In					

	Y0	Y1	Y2	Y3	Y4	Y5
Net Cash Flows						
Cumulative Cash Flow						
Total Profit Improvement						

Net Present Value ($)	
Payback (MOS)	
Return on Investment (%)	

Figure 3-2. Glossary of cost-benefit guidelines.

Investment	Represents customers' total incremental expenditure to obtain our solution, including but over and above their costs to do business with us: capital equipment and materials, software, services other than annual maintenance, training, and other variable costs that will have to be expensed. It is assumed that the total investment is a one-time cost that will be paid out in full in Year 0. Total investment is the ''cost'' in the cost-benefit analysis.
	Multiply the total investment in capital equipment by the current depreciation rate permitted by the accelerated cost recovery schedule (ACRS). Subtract the resulting cash flows generated by cumulative annual depreciation from the total investment.
Cash Flow	Represents the incremental cash benefits generated by the savings and revenues from our solution. They are calculated on a recurrent annual basis that can be accumulated at the end of the useful life of the total investment. Cash flow is the ''benefits'' in the cost-benefit analysis.
Payback	The cumulative cash flows to date have exactly returned the customers' total investments so that they are released from risk and made whole again. After payback, cash flows become positive so that profits can occur.
Net Present Value (NPV)	Represents today's current value of the sum of all the future cash flows after they have been discounted for annual

	opportunity loss based on what the same total investment might have saved or earned if invested elsewhere. Annual opportunity loss is calculated over the useful life of the total investment.
	(The Year One net present value of $50,000 by the time it will be received in Year Two is $41,667, which represents $50,000 discounted by the factor of 0.83333.)
Internal Rate of Return (IRR)	The average annual percent return per dollar invested calculated in discounted dollars. If NPV = $60 at 10 percent cost of capital and if $60 = a rate of return of 8 percent, IRR = 18 percent, (8 percent + 10 percent cost of capital). Cost of capital is the customer's hurdle rate.

being invited to invest in the improvement of the contributions their operations make to their profits—not that they are being asked to buy the consultative seller's products, services, or systems. They have no vested interest in the seller's products. Their only interest is in the assets that they already own and how to improve their contributions.

A project in profit improvement begins when customers close the sellers' proposal. The project ends not with the one-time delivery of products and services but with the on-time delivery of improved customer profits. In between, the sellers must manage the flow of work. Even more important, they must manage the flow of new profits.

The ability to diagnose heretofore unsolved customer problems in such a way that they can now be solved is an enviable asset for a project manager. So is the ability to conceive a simplistic solution that, for the first time, enables a customer problem or opportunity to be dealt with cost-effectively. But the greatest ability is *dependability*. Can the project manager be depended on to control the project, to keep it from getting out of hand, to pick up deviations quickly and remedy them at once, to avoid cost over-runs, and to be free of surprises? If the answers are either no or, even worse, sometimes, no amount of creativity or simplistic problem solving can atone for the absence of reliability.

No two consultative sellers have the same intellectual capital or employ their capital in the same way. Given identical customer operations, customer objectives, and commodity products and services, one consultative seller will always propose what a customer regards as the single best solution—the most cost-effective way of solving a problem or realizing an opportunity. How can you become the proposer of the winning PIP and, consequently, the manager of the winning project?

The secret of Consultative Selling success is your personal ability to come up with an optimal mix of muchness, soonness, and sureness of benefits for each PIP. In other words, how much better than the next consultative seller is your intellectual capital when you apply it to bring together your technology smarts with your process smarts about a customer's operations?

The value basis for Consultative Selling can be summed up in a single sentence: *Consultative sellers are in the business of selling a dollar's worth of value for 50 or 60 cents on the dollar.*

This is more than any vendor can get for selling a dollar's worth of cost.

Selling dollars is crucial because no one can make margin on products anymore. Yotaro Suzuki of the Japan Institute of Office Automation asks, "How do you assign prices in a world where quality is perfect?" Hiroshi Yamauchi of Nintendo concludes that "there is no way to charge a premium on hardware." In the United States, the most common assessment of suppliers by their customers is, "They make a great machine. So what?"

POSITIONING PRODUCT BUSINESSES AS SERVICES

Consultative Selling transforms product businesses into financial service businesses by converting a product's operating values into dollar values—and then selling the dollars, not the product.

Since the dollars are used to improve a customer's profits, the supplier who practices Consultative Selling is providing a service. The name of the service is continuous business improvement of the customer. The role of the supplier's products and processes is to enable the service to realize its objective.

In this way, a product-based business can segue into a service by reversing the rank order of importance of what it makes and how it sells what it makes. It sells as a service. It continues to make products as a manufacturer, but it makes its money on the service of counseling customers how to apply its products to improve their profits.

The business advisory role of a financial service provider allows consultative sellers to make their own products or to buy products from outsourced contract manufacturers. It also allows them to offer the products of other manufacturers with either their proprietary brand names or as no-name "white boxes." It makes no difference because, in any event, the products themselves are not sold. Only their contributions to customer profits are priced and proposed.

Service businesses propose profit improvement in the same manner as product businesses. The cost of providing their service, like the cost of products, is irrelevant as the basis for price as long as it is met. The capital equipment employed—human capital rather than hardware capital—is unique. But it still requires a customer to make an investment in its application, and the investment still requires a positive rate of return to make it compelling.

In examining a cost-benefit analysis, there should be no way to tell if its outcomes are being calculated for a product business, a service business that is being enabled by products, or a service business that is a pure play in which no products at all are involved. The only telltale sign in some cases might be a smaller investment on the cost-benefit's top line and a consequently higher IRR as the result of lower or no hardware capital expenses.

The Consultative Selling service business model can take several forms. Electronic Data Systems (EDS) is a pure service play. It manufactures nothing. As an outsourcer of corporate information systems, EDS sells the results of its services in reducing its customers' costs by getting IT off their books. EDS may also be able to generate revenue from an IT system by managing it more productively and renting out the excess capacity for gains that can be shared with customers.

IBM Global Services is also an outsourcer as well as an IT systems maintenance organization. Like EDS, it sells the value of the improved results it can realize for customers. Many of its own products are embedded in the systems it engineers, operates, and maintains. So are many competitive products such as computers, servers, and printers. IBM professes an ecumenical attitude. It makes its money on sharing in the value of the gains it creates, which are far greater than the margins on sales of hardware, software, or systems.

The decision to engage EDS or IBM is a financial decision. In order to make sense operationally to a customer, it must make or save dollars financially. No less than traditional financial services such as GE Capital or Citigroup, EDS and IBM Global Services represent themselves as sources of funds. If customers want their money, they will show them the costs and the benefits of their strategy for improving access to financial capital. It will come not from lending them new assets but from the service provided by making their current assets more competitive.

Product-based managers have often disparaged service businesses as dealing in intangibles. But the improved customer profits that a service business sells when it employs Consultative Selling strategies are no less tangible than the profits sold by a product manufacturer. They represent hard cash. They can be taken to the bank. They show up as earnings. In the end, profits are the ultimate tangible. From a customer's point of view, their source is far less important than their amount, the speed with which they flow in, and their predictability.

CONSULTATIVE
PARTNERING
STRATEGIES

4

How to Set Partnerable Objectives

In order to grow a customer's business, you must get inside it. *Unless you know it, you cannot grow it.* No business can be grown from the outside. By being an insider, you can be *in business* together with your customer instead of just *doing business* as an outside supplier. The opportunities to be in business together are found in the customer operations, where you can affect outcomes and where growth can take place if you are able to improve them.

Contributing to customer results shows up in one survey after another as one of the top three critical success factors in customer satisfaction. Few customers say that they need better products. Many products exceed customer needs, such as Digital Equipment's "fastest-on-earth" Alpha microprocessor, whose price had to be cut back periodically to compete with the lower-priced, slower systems of Hewlett-Packard and Sun, whose performance was "good enough." What comes across is that customers need supplier performance—not product performance—in three categories: more knowledge of customer operations, more understanding of customer competitive situations and more strategic ways to deal with them, and more proactive contributions to customer profit improvement that are made without having to be asked for.

Customers are the genesis of your business. For this reason, you must both be in the same business. This means that the customer must come first, by making customer profitability your combined prime objective and managing your business as being *of* your customers, *by* your customers, and *for* your customers.

Every business has natural partners. Who are yours? They are other businesses whose growth is dependent on you. Selecting your growth partners is the single most important act of Consultative Selling.

Good partners meet five criteria:

1. They want to grow.
2. They want you to grow them.
3. The growth they want from you is within your norms.
4. They can grow you in return.
5. Their growth by you will convert additional good partners.

If you know who your natural partners are and what they need from you in order to grow, you can dedicate your Profit Improvement Proposals to them from the outset. Your business positioning can be a natural response to theirs. Also, your system capabilities can be exactly receptive to their needs. Furthermore, your database can contain knowledge of their growth problems and opportunities. Your entire business can be the reciprocal of the businesses of your partners.

You have two types of natural growth partners. One is composed of businesses that are currently growing because of you. The other is composed of businesses that you could grow but are not currently growing.

CHOOSING PARTNERABLE CUSTOMERS

There are four questions to answer about your current customers in order to determine which of them you should partner with.

1. *Whom are you growing right now?* Some of your growth partners are customers you are already growing. You may not be aware of your contribution to their growth. You may think you

are merely selling to them. But they are actually partners without portfolio. In order to determine whether any one of them should be selected as your partner, you have to answer three more questions.

2. *How much more can you grow them?* Growth takes place in the future. What is the most likely projected rate of improved profits you can plan for in the growth of their business over the next three years? If the projected rate of growth is static or in decline, you may not have a true growth partner. Instead, you may have a mature customer to whom you can continue to vend products at competitive prices, whom you should sell to and profit from but not partner.

3. *How much are they growing you?* You may be unable to know the full extent to which you are bringing growth to a current customer. But you can much more easily calculate the profits by which you are growing as a result of the customer's business with you. There are four standards by which you should measure profits: their absolute value, their comparative value ranked against your customer list as a whole, their rate of growth, and the trend of their growth rate over the past three years.

4. *How much more can they grow you?* Because growth partnerships must be reciprocal, you must evaluate the most likely projected rate of your own profit growth over the next three years to see whether it is increasing, becoming static, or entering decline. If the projected incremental rates of growth are increasing for both your customer's and your own business, you have the ideal basis for growth partnering.

There are three questions to answer about prospective partners in order to determine which of them you should partner with:

1. *Whom else can you grow?* Growable businesses that you are not currently growing are your source of consultative expansion. In order to qualify as a growable customer, a business must meet two criteria. Its business function problems must be susceptible to significant cost reduction by the application of your expertise. In addition, your expertise must be able to increase the customer's own profitable sales opportunities.

2. How can you grow them? For each growable customer that you determine is potentially partnerable, you must plan a growth strategy. The strategy will set forth the precise means by which you will add new profits to the customer's business. You will need to specify how much profit will accrue from reducing business function costs, how soon its flow will begin, and how long it will continue. You will also have to specify the amount and flow of profit from new sales opportunities that you can make available and the markets they can be expected to come from.

3. How much will they grow you? A business that you can grow must be able to grow you in return if it is to be partnerable. Its contribution to your profit volume and its projected three-year rate of growth must meet or exceed your company's minimum growth requirements.

When it comes to gainsharing, not all partnerships are created equally conducive. Gainsharing represents the essence of partnering, where rewards are shared in proportion to risk and contribution. Relationships that, for one reason or another, stop short of profit sharing are stopping short of full partnering.

"Full Monty" partnerships of total comity meet selective criteria. These criteria allow partnerships to be assessed with a good deal of predictability. Some criteria are personal to the customer partners: Are they natural sharers by personality or self-aggrandizing nongivers? Are they predisposed to think in terms of benefits or their costs? Are they dealmakers or traditionalists about price being the sole basis for transactions?

"Know your customer" means to know these things. Over and above them are situational factors that may modify or nullify personal criteria. They include:

- A business that wants or needs to be first to apply a new technology, either because it is a leader and wants to stay that way or because it must get closer to the leader.
- A business that is cash poor and cannot pay for the benefits it needs.
- A young business that must conserve cash for growth but needs every accelerant to growth that it can get its hands on.

- A business whose industry is in an economic downturn and can use gainsharing as a form of barter to trade present uplift for a future payment.
- A business in a highly competitive industry that cannot risk a negative impact on its stock price from a major cash outlay on its balance sheet.

For businesses in any of these situations, selectively used gainsharing can be an incremental growth strategy. Depending on a customer's position in its industry, its market, or its life cycle, partnerability may be more dependent on the speed with which gain can be created than by its total amount. Fast gain can make fast partners. It can also predispose negotiations to yield a favorable share for the consultative seller.

CYCLING CONTINUOUS IMPROVEMENT

How can you tell if customer managers are partners? If they give you leads by telling you where they hurt or what unrealized opportunities they fantasize about, they are partners. If they keep asking you, what next? or, what else can you do for us? or, where do we go from here? after each successful PIP project, they are partners. If they sell for you by going upstairs to get funds for your PIPs, they are partners.

A continuous improvement cycle is composed of consecutive PIPs. Each successive PIP is initiated while the preceding PIP is no more than halfway into its projected life. As soon as PIP #1 produces profits, a share of its gains can be allocated to fund a part or all of the investment required by PIP #2, and so on.

As PIP self-funding proceeds, a "partners' pool of funds" is created for you to draw on. This is the ultimate outcome of your partnering—a partnership that capitalizes itself to achieve financial autonomy, free from the need for third-party sponsorship of its investments in continuous profit improvement.

A business partnership is legitimized only when a partners' pool of funds is created. Up to that point, it is merely a relationship. Once a pool of funds is capitalized by the partners, they can dip into it at their discretion as if they were a miniature business. The customer manager ceases to be a customer and becomes a *client*. The consultative seller ceases to be a seller and becomes a *comanager*.

Partnering requires two choices. One is your selection of the customers you will grow. The second is made by your customers: Why should they partner with you? There are three reasons:

1. *You are an important source of their growth profits*. The contribution of new profits that you can make to customers must be significant. Only then will your partnership be important enough to both of you to merit top-of-the-mind attention, both theirs and yours.

To be an important source of growth for customers means that you must account for worthwhile incremental profits. You must also be able to deliver them in a timely fashion, recognizing the time value that money has for them. In this, you must be dependable. They must be able to count on you to improve their profits when you say you will and by the amounts you promise. Your importance to them will be in direct proportion to your reliability.

2. *You are one of their best investments in continuous profit growth*. When partners do business with you, they must perceive the price they pay to be an investment rather than a cost. The distinction is vital, because only an investment yields a return. They must understand that they are not investing in your products or services or systems, not even in your solutions. They will be investing in new profits. The return they receive from their investment with you must be among the best yields they can make.

Just how high do customers' returns on investing with you have to be? You must compare yourself with their options. Normally customers will invest in their own business in order to make profits. They have a "hurdle rate" that sets their minimum return. As their partner, you must offer them a better choice. You must make it more profitable for them to invest in your business. Either the investment they are required to make will be smaller yet yield a similar or faster return, or the return they receive from you will be larger, even though the investment may also be correspondingly larger.

3. *You both have the same competitors.* When you sell products or services, positioning yourself as one of a customer's several alternate vendors, you are concerned only with defeating your own competitors—rival vendors. To be a business partner means that you must concentrate on defeating your *customer's competitors.* Unless you have the same objective, you cannot be partners.

Customers' competitors are the constraints on their growth. They have two of them. One is their current costs, against which they compete every day and which they must reduce if they are to improve their profits. You must help them. Their second source of competition is in the area of sales opportunities. They compete for them every day too, trying to win customers against their competition. If they are going to improve their profits, they must increase their profitable market penetration. You must help them.

As your partners, your customers grow you if you can make three transformations in your relationships with them.

You must first transform yourself from a supplier of products and services to a supplier of profits. You must change from a manufacturing or service business into a supplier whose product is profits.

You must transform yourself from representing an added cost to representing continuous added value. You must change your basis for doing business from selling performance values at a price to returning dollar values on an investment. Otherwise, you may never have the chance to partner.

Pressurizing the Partnering Prerogative

Ever since product and service commoditization became legislated by customer insistence on open standards, supplier control has been inevitable as a logical extension of customer dominion over supply chain management. The PICOS program of General Motors shows how product-based vendors are being pressured to relinquish their partnering prerogative.

PICOA stands for GM's Program for the Improvement and Cost Optimization of Suppliers, a politically correct manner of describing the continuing thrust to reduce the costs of all the parts that go into each GM car.

1. Overall Strategy
   a. Get immediate price reductions.
   b. Secure longer-term price reductions from all suppliers
   c. Sort out the first and second tier suppliers.
   d. Only single source with significant price reductions (18 to 40 percent) that are firmly baked into fixed-price, long-term contracts.
2. Tactical Overview
   a. Establish well-qualified, well-trained, and articulate purchasing clones in all business units to implement these practices.
   b. Plan extensive supplier price reductions for each car model.
   c. Send out inquiries around the world in search of the lowest unit price.
   d. Establish short- and long-term price reduction targets and go very low.
   e. Know your potential winning suppliers and their competitors inside and out before you begin to negotiate and play first and second tier suppliers against each other.
3. The Underlying Themes
   a. Identify and parade the enemy as Japanese companies, not GM.
   b. Understand the balance of power between each supplier and GM.
   c. Keep taking the temperature with vendor ratings and supplier council meetings.
   d. Offer exaggerated growth and future order quantities as bonuses.
   e. Start working with the likely winning suppliers as early as possible on price reductions that are termed "cost reductions improvements."

4. Before Awarding the Deals
   a. Establish long-term contracts as the ultimate goal.
   b. Establish the long-term contract rules.
   c. Establish that nonprice factors like tooling costs and R&D are not allowed.
   d. Resist all suggestions that some supplier costs are not controllable (i.e., raw materials).
   e. Focus all activity on dramatically and immediately reducing the unit price.
5. The Agreements
   a. Tie up the short-term unit price.
   b. Keep nibbling away at the price and terms even at the midnight hour.
   c. Always appear to be in a desperate hurry, but in reality take as much time as needed.
   d. Pull the long-term deal out of the cupboard.
   e. Intensely squeeze some more out.
   f. Get the supplier to sign.
6. Managing the Chosen Suppliers
   a. Introduce the suppliers to our corporate commodity councils and our advanced purchasing product development teams.
   b. Totally involve each supplier's top and upper management—get commitments that the supplier's middle management would never make.
   c. Request that each supplier provide you with detailed information on the cost-profit structure of the products it currently or proposes to sell us.
   d. Don't accept raw material indexes as cost information when a supplier proposes a price increase; get the cost-profit information.
   e. Establish a friend-buddy relationship with middle and lower-level supplier people to pass cost-profit and competitive information to us.
   f. Be prepared indirectly and under pressure to bluff.
   g. Destabilize each supplier's people with many urgent meetings and many demands for information.

h. Set new deadlines for suppliers to meet but defer decisions to increase their anxiety.

PICOS programs are becoming epidemic. As they proliferate, their impact is becoming predictable. A supplier's margins go first, followed by investment in R&D, plant and equipment, and in the sales force. Noncore assets are cut back and outsourced and the number and quality of supplies that go into a product are cut down.

SATISFYING RISK AVERSION

Risk tolerance is a highly personalized trait. The commitment of customer managers to invest in a PIP is always a trade-off between their perception of risk and the PIP's potential profits. No matter how many dollars of profits you propose, managers will adjust them downward for risk. This reflects the managers' subjective sense of the unlikelihood of their realization: in other words, their estimate of uncertainty about the future.

All PIPs deal in futures. The faster the future payoff, the more certain the PIP. As the time frame to payback and payout lengthens, customer managers have a more difficult task in forecasting the probability of PIP success. The same characteristics that make the PIP so successful can also make its customers' evaluations more intense:

- Each PIP focuses on a single best solution, ruling out contingencies.
- Each PIP focuses on a single factor that is critical to the success of a customer operation or sales to a market segment, eliminating options.

The space between a PIP's proposal of realizable future profits and the costs of uncertainty is known as its "trade space." It is the space within which customers contain their indecision, their yes-no trading area where they go back and forth in their decision-making process. Invest in these prospective profits or not? Invest this much, more, or less? Invest now or accept this much opportunity cost? Live with this much technological uncertainty or this much market volatility?

After adjusting a PIP's profits for risk as customer managers perceive it, they place a personalized dollar value on the PIP's stream of cash flows. From this moment on, the PIP's value is contingent on the managers' sense of how much any uncertainty may cost. The resolution of this calculation will become the PIP's negotiable net worth.

Since minimizing risk automatically inflates a PIP's perceived value, you should ask yourself how much you are willing to invest to reduce risk: that is, to shrink the customer's trade space so you can get to close fast. Three investment opportunities are available to you:

1. Guarantee the PIP's payout. This means that you pay any default between your proposed value and the customer's realized value so that the customer is made whole.

2. Insure the PIP's payout. This means that a third-party insurer pays any default to the customer, but you pay premiums to the insurer.

3. Gainshare in the PIP's payout. This means that you share in some or all of the customer's risk by depending for your own compensation on the reward. You can claim a larger share of the gain if you are willing to put up some or all of the up-front costs.

Even without accepting the added burden of taking on the risk of partnering with a supplier, customers are already inundated with risk factors in their own businesses. They include the unpredictability of their operating results, the uncertainty associated with the introduction of new products, the exposure they feel from their dependence on a small number of currently successful products and markets, the potential failure to manage their growth and avoid compliance liabilities or a loss of proprietary rights, and the chance that they may be unable to raise capital if they need it. The following statements of risk by a semiconductor equipment manufacturer are typical of the dangers that all customers deal with even before a supplier knocks on their doors.

Our Quarterly Revenues and Operating Results are Unpredictable

Our revenues and operating results may fluctuate significantly from quarter to quarter due to a number of factors, not all of which are in our control. These factors include:

- Economic conditions in the semiconductor industry generally, and the equipment industry specifically
- Customer capacity requirements
- The size and timing of orders from customers
- Customer cancellations or delays in our shipments
- Our ability in a timely manner to develop, introduce, and market new, enhanced, and competitive products
- Legal or technical challenges to our products and technology
- Changes in average selling prices and product mix
- Exchange rate fluctuations

We base our expense levels in part on our expectations of future revenues. If revenue levels in a particular quarter do not meet our expectations, our operating results are adversely affected.

Further, because of our continuing consolidation of manufacturing operations, natural, physical, logistical or other events or disruptions could adversely impact our financial performance.

We Are Dependent Upon a Limited Number of Key Suppliers.

We obtain certain components and sub-assemblies included in our products from a single supplier or a limited group of suppliers. Each of our key suppliers has a one-year blanket purchase contract under which we may issue purchase orders. We may renew these contracts periodically. Each of these suppliers sold us products during at least the last four years, and we expect that we will continue to renew these contracts in the future or that we will otherwise replace them with competent alternative source suppliers. We believe that we could obtain alternative sources to supply these products. Nevertheless, a prolonged inability to obtain certain components could adversely affect our operating results and result in damage to our customer relationships.

We Depend on New Products and Processes for Our Success. For This Reason, We Are Subject to Risks Associated with Rapid Technological Change.

Rapid technological changes in semiconductor manufacturing processes subject us to increased pressure to maintain technological parity with deep submicron process technology. We believe that our future success depends in part upon our ability to develop, manufacture and introduce successfully new products and product lines with improved capabilities, and to continue to enhance our existing products. Due to the risks inherent in transitioning to new products, we must forecast accurately demand for new products while managing the transition from older products. If new products have reliability or quality problems, reduced orders, higher manufacturing costs, delays in acceptance of and payment for new products and additional service and warranty expenses may result. In the past, product introductions caused some delays and reliability and quality problems. We may be unable to develop and manufacture new products successfully, or new products that we introduce may fail in the marketplace, which would materially and adversely affect our results from operations.

We Are Subject to Risks Relating to Product Concentration and Lack of Product Revenue Diversification.

We derive a substantial percentage of our revenues from a limited number of products, and we expect these products to continue to account for a large percentage of our revenues in the near term. Continued market acceptance of our primary products is, therefore, critical to our future success. Our business, operating results, financial condition and cash flows could therefore be adversely affected by:

- A decline in demand for our products
- A failure to achieve continued market acceptance of our products
- An improved version of products being offered by a competitor in the market we participate in
- Technological change which we are unable to match in our products
- A failure to release new enhanced versions of our products on a timely basis

Our Ability to Manage Potential Growth, Integration of Potential Acquisitions, and Potential Disposition of Product Lines and Technologies Creates Risks for Us.

Our management may face significant challenges in improving financial and business controls, management processes, information systems and procedures on a timely basis, and expanding, training and managing our work force if we experience additional growth. There can be no assurance that we will be able to perform such actions successfully. In the future, we may make additional acquisitions of complementary companies, products or technologies, or we may reduce or dispose of certain product lines or technologies, which no longer complement our long-term strategy. Managing an acquired business or disposing of product technologies entails numerous operational and financial risks, including difficulties in assimilating acquired operations and new personnel or separating existing business or product groups, diversion of management's attention to other business concerns, amortization of acquired intangible assets and potential loss of key employees or customers of acquired or disposed operations. There can be no assurance that we will be able to achieve and manage effectively any such growth, integration of potential acquisitions or disposition of product lines or technologies, or that our management, personnel or systems will be adequate to support continued operations. Any such inabilities or inadequacies would have a material and adverse effect on our business, operating results, financial condition and cash flows.

Intellectual Property and Other Claims Against Us Can be Costly and Could Result in the Loss of Significant Rights That Are Necessary to Our Continued Business and Profitability.

Other parties may assert infringement, unfair competition or other claims against us. Additionally, from time to time, other parties send us notices alleging that our products infringe their patent or other intellectual property rights. In such cases, it is our policy either to defend the claims or to negotiate licenses on commercially reasonable terms. However, we may be unable in the future to negotiate necessary licenses on commercially reasonable terms, or at all, and any litigation resulting from these claims by other parties may materially adversely affect our business and financial results.

We May Fail to Protect Our Proprietary Technology Rights, Which Would Affect Our Business.

Our success depends in part on our proprietary technology. While we attempt to protect our proprietary technology through patents, copyrights and trade secret protection, we believe that our success depends on increasing our technological expertise, continuing our development of new systems, increasing market penetration and growth of our installed base, and providing comprehensive support and service to our customers. However, we may be unable to protect our technology in all instances, or our competitors may develop similar or more competitive technology independently. Other parties may challenge or attempt to invalidate or circumvent any patents the United States or foreign governments issue to us or these governments may fail to issue pending applications. In addition, the rights granted or anticipated under any of these patents or pending patent applications may be narrower than we expect or in fact provide no competitive advantages.

5

How to Agree on
Partnerable Strategies

Aconsultant's job can be defined in three ways: Bring back
sales, bring back customer information that can lead to sales, and
leave behind alliances with top-tier decision makers.

Sometimes a sale will build an alliance. More often, alliances
help build sales.

There are four levels on which alliances must be structured in
a key customer account. Three of them are in the upper management tier: top managers, financial managers, and operating managers. The fourth is the purchasing level, where the traditional
adversary relationship must be converted into a more partnerable
affiliation.

The objectives of all key account alliances are similar, regardless of the level at which they are to be achieved. Their overriding
goal is to ensure customer continuity. Unless key account relationships are continuous, there will be no way to maximize the profit
opportunity that a major customer represents. Unless you can keep
your key customers, everything else is academic.

Making Mutually Profitable Alliances

Three strategies will help you build lasting alliances: Collaborate, educate, and negotiate.

1. *Collaborate.* In key account situations, it takes two to
make every sale. An unpartnered consultant cannot sell within a

customer's company. There will be no one to sell *to*. There will be no one to sell *with*. There will be no one to *help sell*. For consultant and collaborator, there must be the same dedication, the same commitment, and the same conviction that a sale will add genuine value to both parties. When a sale is finally made, it should be impossible to tell who made it. This is the test of a true collaboration: The sale is the thing, not the seller.

2. *Educate.* You and your key customers must do more than buy and sell if your relationships are to be continuous. Along with making new dollars, you should both be making new information available to the people on each side who will be collaborating on proposing sales. Not only must you both *earn* as a result of your relationships, you must both *learn* as well. Professional growth and personal growth should attend profit growth.

3. *Negotiate.* The main subject area of the mutual education between collaborators is how to improve profits. This requires continuing back-and-forth dialogue. The flow of input must be unimpeded. The ideal environment is rich in options but sparse in negative thinking, put-downs, editorializing, or defensiveness against anything that is "not invented here." Free-swinging relationships where there is a high degree of give-and-take allow you and your customers to avoid losing out on important opportunities. They also allow you to cash in fully on solving the problems that come off the top of the customer's head.

Alliances with Top Managers

By selling as a consultant, you can obtain access up and down the entire vertical chain of a customer's C-level organization, including the chief operating officer, who is usually the president, and the chief financial officer. If you sell to a division or subsidiary of a large customer company, your top allies may be its COO and CFO. Selling to several divisions or to the corporate management itself will require you to partner at the top company level of chief executive officer as well as at top divisional levels.

Alliances with Middle Managers

For the most part, your alliances will be at Box Two midlevels of cost centers and line-of-business profit centers.

At the profit center level, you will be partnering with two different types of business managers: those who run *margin businesses* and others who run *turnover businesses*. Each type requires its own partnership strategy. At the same time, you will also be partnering with cost center managers who service, support, and supply the lines of business.

1. *Partnering with margin business managers.* A margin business makes money on high profit per unit of sale. Most margin businesses are brand businesses, smaller rather than larger, and serve niche markets. A small improvement in volume for a margin business can yield a large increase in profits. When you PIP margin business managers, propose to increase their sales revenues without raising their variable costs or propose to reduce their variable costs without having an adverse effect on their revenues.

2. *Partnering with turnover business managers.* A turnover business makes money on high volume. Most turnover businesses are commodity businesses, larger rather than smaller, and serve mass markets. A large improvement in volume for a turnover business is required to yield significantly improved profits. When you PIP turnover business managers, propose to increase their sales revenues while keeping operating funds requirements constant or reducing them. Alternatively, you can propose to reduce operating funds requirements, as long as you do not reduce revenues. Operating funds requirements can be reduced by cutting down on current variable costs or by displacing some of them by leasing or outsourcing assets instead of purchasing them.

Improving cycle times of a turnover business, such as its time to market or its order fulfillment rate, are the most cost-effective strategies to improve its manager's performance. By speeding up cycle times, you can increase the amount of goods shipped and billed. This speeds up cash flow without having to increase sales volume by increasing the speed of collecting accounts payable. Accelerating the order fulfillment cycle also reduces inventory costs by cutting down on the amount of funds that are tied up in working assets. Accelerating collections cuts down further on the same funds. Each operating cycle that you speed up improves productivity by reducing a manager's unit costs of labor and materials.

3. *Partnering with cost center managers.* A cost center manager is preoccupied with running an operation in the most cost-effective manner based on best practices, TQM (total quality management), continuous innovation, and JIT (just-in-time) inventory. Cost center managers in R&D, manufacturing, engineering, marketing, information systems, and human resources are always being measured by their contributions to cost. As a result, work flows and cycle times are key indicators of performance for them. Wasted materials, wasted time, and wasted money are constant targets for improvement.

Opportunities to apply Consultative Selling strategies to customer cost reduction are expanding in proportion to the expanded needs of customers to strive ceaselessly toward the holy grail of zero cost. While variable costs are always the preferred targets for PIPping, at Boeing, as at many other capital-intensive businesses, "We treat every cost, whether fixed or not, as variable and challenge them."

Philip Condit, Boeing's CEO, has linked cost containment to each manager's KPIs. Each facility is charged for the cost of its inventories in computing the economic return of a unit. "All of our bonus and incentive programs key off on this computed economic return." All of the profit-improvement propositions of Boeing's suppliers should do the same.

AGREEING THROUGH NEGOTIATION

Negotiation is the agreement style that partners use. It is designed to make sure that every partner wins something and that no partner loses everything. If any of the partners come away without a win, they have not been negotiated with; they have been commandeered. They have been mastered, not partnered.

What is it that each partner in a partnered negotiation must win? Each must win new, improved profits. Customer partners must have their profits improved by coming away with a lowered cost or higher revenues or earnings. Supplier partners must have their profits improved by coming away with a lowered cost of sale and a higher margin.

In vendor selling, negotiation centers on price. As soon as a price is proposed, discounting begins. Vendors often mistake this process for negotiation. They call it "negotiating price" when they really mean "discounting price." Discounting price is not negotiation because the suppliers cannot win. They can only limit their losses. If their margins are not directly attacked, they will be subjected to other forms of price pressure such as requests for free goods and services, advertising or promotion allowances, free carrying of inventory, and so on.

Because price does not exist in Consultative Selling, partners do not include it in their dialogues. Instead, they negotiate about the yield from the consultative substitute for price: investment. *How much* can it earn? *How soon* can it start to flow? *How sure* can we be—how can we be even surer—that we will receive the muchness we have planned as soon as we have planned for it?

These are the three subjects of partnered negotiation. Both partners want to maximize the sureness of their deals together. Without sureness, everything else is fanciful; Profit Improvement Proposals will be fiction, like a midsummer night's dream. Within the constraints that sureness imposes on the partners, how much return can they manage from their investments, and how soon can they hold it in their hands?

In your role as a consultative seller, you must always be ready to propose more muchness or soonness. The way you do this is by constant what-ifing: What if we add this positive value to our proposal: What effect will we have on return? What if we subtract this negative value from our proposal: What effect will we have on return? With PIPWARE, each option takes only a minute to answer.

The best partnerships consistently earn the highest returns from their investments. They realize that each of them is making an investment of money, time, and resources, and that each must maximize its payoff. As a result, it is not just the consultative partner who proposes and the customer partner who disposes. Both propose to add the maximum value to their mutual proposals. Both what-if each other so that their proposals are true joint ventures. Joint proposals, in which each partner is invested both personally and professionally, are the outcomes of partnered negotiation.

If you are asked how you know you are practicing partnered negotiation, a joint Profit Improvement Proposal is not only your best answer; it is your only answer.

SEPARATING PARTNERS FROM NONPARTNERS

Every decision maker can be considered as a fraction. The denominator is always the same: common needs and aspirations. Every numerator, though, is exceptional; numerators are composed of individual differences. In order to penetrate a customer organization, you have to analyze what is individual as well as what is common. This can be done by answering two questions: "Who are the decision makers I can partner with?" "Who are the decision makers I will have difficulty partnering with?"

Decision Makers Who Make Good Partners

There are six types of decision makers who have high partnering potential. Figure 5-1 summarizes their principal characteristics and most probable negotiating modes.

Decision Makers Who Make Difficult Partners

There are six types of decision makers who have low partnering potential. Figure 5-2 summarizes their principal characteristics and most probable negotiating modes.

Consultative Selling enables sustainable commercial relationships. As long as a customer manager's profit contribution is being improved by a consultative seller, they can continue to grow each other as "partners in profits."

Consultative sellers do not make calls. They make projects that can migrate from one profit contribution to the next so that the seller's initial cost of sale is amortized over infinity. Nor do consultative sellers transact business through finite, sporadic engagements. Instead, they become partners in perpetuity. As long as managers have a line of business or a business function to run, their profit contributions are always susceptible to improvement, just as their KPIs are always made more stringent and less readily achievable.

The traditional product vendor skills of maximizing the number of calls per day in order to sell something to everybody have no place in Consultative Selling. The same is true for the service vendor skills of selling finite engagements whose termination, no matter how successful, more often than not leaves their vendors back where they were: on the street to start all over again.

The selling in Consultative Selling should take place once, at the beginning of each partnership, when PIP number one must be agreed on. From then on, the principle of capital turnover should act as the flywheel of each relationship so that its cash flow never stops. The benefits of continuity of turnover—PIP turnover, customer capital turnover, and the seller's turnover of customer investments—compose the added values of partnering. Once a partnership gets up to speed, the seller's cost of sales and sales cycle time should approximate zero. So should the customer partner's cost of acquiring new profit opportunities from the seller.

Partners who are brought together by Consultative Selling gain new money together. But that is not all. They also gain in the time value of their new cash flows. Funds can be earned or saved faster. They can be reinvested faster. There are more funds to reinvest each period because they become available sooner. This is where the payoff of Consultative Selling comes from.

IMPROVING THE ODDS ON "ONE AND IT'S DONE"

You can improve the odds on achieving "one and it's done" partnering efficiency—the Six Sigma of Consultative Selling—by taking two factors into account before you commit to a PIP's creation:

- The customer manager's actual and potential "What elses?"
- The manager's actual and potential "Why Nots?"

As your partnerships mature, what elses and why nots become easier for you to know, either experientially because you are

Figure 5-1. High-partnering decision makers.

Manager Type	Characteristics	Negotiation Modes
Bureaucrat	Rational, formal, impersonal, disciplined, jealous of rights and prerogatives of office, well-versed in organizational politics.	Follows rules; stickler for compliance; more concerned with tasks than with people; logical strategist (but can be a nitpicker); predictable negotiator.
Zealot	Competent loner, impatient, outspoken, a nuisance to bureaucrats, insensitive to others, minimal political skills.	Devoted to good of organization; aggressive and domineering negotiator; blunt and direct; totally task-oriented.
Executive	Dominant but not domineering, directive but permits freedom, consultative but not participative, sizes up people well but relates only on a surface level, cordial but at arm's length.	Organization-oriented; high task concentration; assertive negotiator; adroit strategist; flexible and resourceful.

(continues)

Figure 5-1. (Continued).

Integrator	Egalitarian, supportive, participative, excellent interpersonal skills, a born team builder, a catalyst who is adept at unifying conflicting values.	Shares leadership; permits freedom of decisions and delegates authority; welcomes ideas; open and honest negotiator who seeks win-win relationships.
Gamesperson	Fast-moving, flexible, upward-moving, impersonal, risk taker, one convinced that winning is everything, innovative, opportunistic but ethical, plays the game fairly but will give nothing away.	Wants to win every negotiation; enjoys competition of ideas, jockeying for position, and maneuvers of the mind; sharp, skilled, and tough negotiator; can be a win-win strategist.
Autocrat	Paternalistic, patronizing, closed to new ideas that are not invented here, not consultative or participative, but partnerable on own terms.	Binds people emotionally; rules from position of authority; makes pronouncements of policy; a sharp trader who negotiates on a tit-for-tat basis.

Figure 5-2. Low-partnering decision makers.

Manager Type	Characteristics	Negotiation Modes
Machiavellian	Self-oriented, shrewd, devious, and calculating, insightful into weaknesses of others, opportunistic, suave and charismatic, can turn in an instant from collaboration to aggression.	An exploiter of people; cooperates only for selfish interests; totally impersonal negotiator, unmoved by human appeals; will win as inexpensively as possible, but will win at all costs.
Missionary	Smoother of conflict, blender of ideas, must be liked, identifies harmony with acceptance, highly subjective and personal.	A seeker of compromise and leveler of ideas to lowest common denominator; negotiates emotionally with personal appeals to agree for own sake.
Exploiter	Arrogant, what's-in-it-for-me attitude, coercive, domineering, rigid, prejudiced, takes advantage of weakness, makes snap judgments, unswayed by evidence.	Exerts constrictive personal control over negotiation; makes others vulnerable by using pressure and fear to get own way; demands subservience; sees others as obstacles to be overcome.

(continues)

Figure 5-2. (Continued).

Climber	Striving, driving, smooth and polished demeanor that masks aggression, opportunistic, without loyalty to others, goes with flow.	Excellent politician; uses self-propelling change to call attention to self; always thinking ahead; self-serving negotiator based on what-will-this-do-for-me?
Conserver	Defends status quo, resists change, favors evolutionary improvement, uses the system skillfully to safeguard personal position and prerogatives.	Imposes own sense of order and nonimmediacy on negotiation; slows everything down; preaches traditional values; defensively blocks innovation and undermines agreements before implementation.
Glad-hander	Superficially friendly to new ideas but essentially a nondoer, effusive, socially skilled and politically skillful, superior survival instincts.	Overreactive and overstimulated by everything but impressed by little; promises support but then fades away; endorses only sure things that can do some personal good; never takes risks.

exposed to them in the course of your relationships or intuitively based on knowing your partners. At the outset of new relationships, however, you may have to ask; unasked or unanswered, you may have to reason your way to go–no go decisions about PIPping.

Assaying the "what elses" means learning the customer managers' investment options, the claims that the managers, their top managers, or suppliers of competitive options may have made on the funds you would like to stake out for yourself. Rival claims come from three main sources:

1. A mandate from upstairs that freezes funds for a use that top management regards as critical to the success of the business. This may entail a performance improvement in the direction of best practices, an acquisition to fill a gap in a product line, or a reallocation of resources to beef up services at the expense of products.

2. A priority that gets funded first because it is a hotter button than your hot button. This may be a personal quest on the part of a manager that makes equal subjective as well as economic sense. Or it may be an investment that a manager must make to safeguard a previously funded initiative, such as an upgrading renovation or repair.

3. A better offer that has a more compelling return in terms of its muchness, soonness, or sureness. Such an offer does not need to be directly competitive with your own proposition in either its application or choice of operational function. It needs only to challenge for similar funds at a similar level of risk in order to be competitive.

Assaying the "why nots" means learning customer managers' investment constraints that are outside their priorities and hurdle rates. Constraints, most of which are self-imposed, come from two main sources:

1. A lack of sufficient sureness to proceed. Uncertainty may come from concern that your proposed profit improvement is too small to be worthwhile or too large to be credible. This constraint

may be overcome by guaranteeing the proposed results and reducing up-front cost as much as possible by gainsharing.

2. A heightened sense of risk. Commitment may be inhibited by concern that exposure to forfeiture of principal is too high or that a protracted delay in its recovery is a signal of eventual forfeiture. This constraint may be overcome by reducing the time to payback, either by cutting back on the amount of funds invested in year zero or accelerating the flow of benefits.

Fast closing your PIPs the first time every time is essential to maximizing the net present value of the technology that enables their outcomes. It is therefore directly related to the margins you can claim in return for the value you add. PIPs that encounter delay add to their cost of sale and to your customers' cost of acquisition. Similarly, PIPs that end up as scrap incur opportunity cost for both of you. This gives sellers and customers alike a vested interest in maintaining a "one and it's done" turnover schedule.

6

How to Ensure
Partnerable Rewards

You and your support staff are the essential partnering
agents in Consultative Selling. Together, you compose a profit-
improvement team for each of your customers. You, the consultant, are the leader of the team. You will partner with the customer
business function managers whose costs you can reduce and with
the managers of the customer's lines of business whose sales can
be increased. The minimal resources you need as team leader and
their relationship to you are shown in Figure 6-1.

Three types of support from within your company will be
essential: financial, data, and technical. All supportive team mem-
bers will play two roles. Internally, within the team, they will
coach and counsel you in preparing and presenting Profit Improvement Proposals, as well as implementing them. Externally, they
will create partnerships with their correlates in the customer's
business—finance to finance, data to data, technical to technical.

Your first act as consultant should be to form your profit-
improvement teams on a customer-by-customer basis. Your second act is to consult with your clients on the organization of com-
panion teams composed of their own staff resources. As Figure
6-2 shows, a client team is built around the decision makers who
will be your partners. By melding the two teams, you create your
partnership.

In Figure 6-1 you must be able to see yourself in the box
marked "Consultant Comanager." This will enable you to be the
partner in charge of your team. As such, you will be a playing

Figure 6-1. Supplier profit-improvement team.

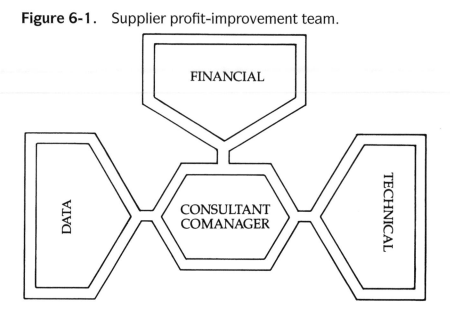

Figure 6-2. Client profit-improvement team.

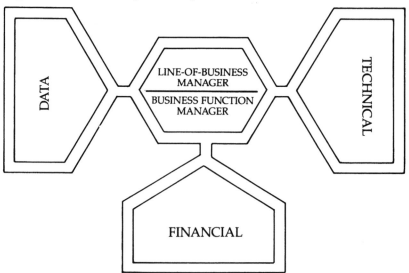

coach, a manager who also plays a position, charged with setting each profit project's objectives and the most cost-effective strategy for achieving them.

PARTNERING ON COMMON DENOMINATORS

All partnering is based on a few common denominators:

- Partners have a *common objective*. Each partner wants to improve profit.
- Partners have *common strategies* for achieving their objective. Their methods are based on mutual need-seeking and mutual need-fulfillment. In both cases, needs are arrived at through negotiation.
- Partners are at *common risk*. Each partner has something of value to gain or lose.
- Partners have a *common defense* against all others who are not included in the partnership. Each party deals as an equal. Outsiders range from being less equal to being perceived as competitors.

Cooperative negotiation strategies enable partners to treat each other as equals. This is the principal rule of partnerships. There are ten additional rules that can help in partnering:

1. *Add value to each other.* Teach each other new ways to improve personal achievement and professional productivity so that both partners profit by the relationship.
2. *Be supportive of each other, not competitive.* Form a staunch team.
3. *Avoid surprises.* Plan work together and work according to plan.
4. *Be open and aboveboard.* Always level with each other.
5. *Enter into each other's frame of reference.* Learn each other's perceptions in order to see things from the other's point of view. Learn each other's assumptions to understand the other's expectations of the partnership.

6. *Be reliable.* Partners must be there for each other when they are needed.

7. *Anticipate opportunities and capitalize on them.* Forecast problems and steer the partnership around them. Keep the partnership out of trouble. If trouble is unavoidable, give the partnership a head start in solving it.

8. *Do homework.* Know what's happening. Know what may happen.

9. *Treat each other as people, not just as functionaries.* Be willing to provide the personal "little extras" that make a partnership a humane as well as a mighty force.

10. *Enjoy the relationship and make it enjoyable.* Both partners should prefer to work within the partnership rather than within any other relationship because it is one of the most rewarding associations either of them has ever had.

The customer decision makers who must be partnered as clients are multimotivated. They rarely act on the basis of one motive alone. Status, money, autonomy, and self-realization propel them. Of all their drives, three are likely to be major: power, achievement, and affiliation.

Client Need Set

In Figure 6-3, three aspects of client needs are illustrated in typical proportion. They contrast with the proportions shown in Figure 6-4 for the consultant's need set. The major difference lies in the relative significance of self-actualization income and psychic income. For the consultant, self-actualization must always take precedence over the psychic rewards of power, prestige, and promotion. For the client, however, you should assume that power and promotion—which represent realizable objectives for a client—supersede self-fulfillment. By remembering the primacy of power and promotion when you negotiate, you will be able to keep your client's perspective in mind. You will also be able to visualize your role fairly accurately in the way the client sees it: to help the client obtain increased power income and maximize money income as well.

Figure 6-3. Client need set.

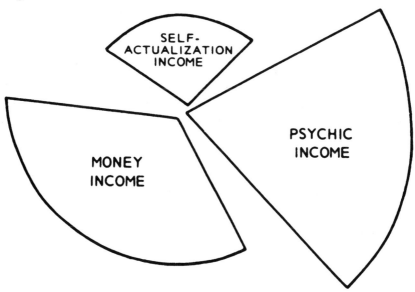

Consultant Need Set

There are three aspects of consultant needs. Each represents a certain type of income: *money income; psychic income,* representing such rewards as power, prestige, and promotion; and *self-actualization income,* including self-fulfillment, competence, and the realization of talent potential.

These needs are present in every consultant's motivation set. Yet they vary widely from one consultant to another. To negotiate effectively, your need set must be proportioned something like Figure 6-4. The money drive you have should be significant. But your use of it to give you power, especially the power to dictate solutions or appropriate a client's leadership, should be small. Although you may enjoy great prestige, you will always be required to work through your client to accomplish your purposes. You can help a client achieve power and promotion and thereby share vicariously in them. But you will often work unheralded, usually anonymously.

On the other hand, consultants must have an unusually large amount of self-actualization in their need set. This aspect is the

Figure 6-4. Consultant need set.

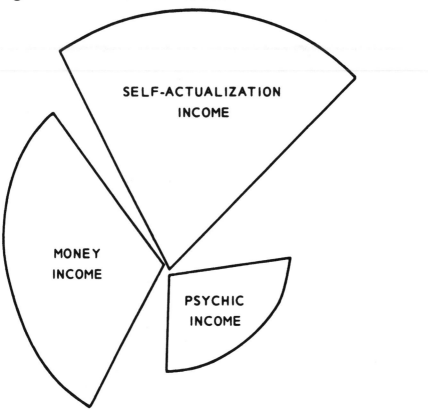

key to success. You must have, and be driven by, a need to realize your own fullest growth and development by growing and developing your client partners. You must want to utilize all of yourself in your clients' behalf, engaging your full complement of skills and expressing your widest range of knowledge. You must need to translate these qualities into unique profit projects that only they and they alone should ever know have originated with you.

PREDICTING PARTNERABILITY

Before admitting you into partnership, a customer manager screens you through a checklist like this:

- What is the *reward*—can they produce what they propose within the time they have proposed it?
- How much will it *cost* to educate them in my operation?
- How much *disruption* will it cause if I bring them in? What is the most likely interruption to my people's productivity?
- What is the *risk* of sharing my priorities and proprietary objectives with them?

You can predict your own partnerability by evaluating yourself against a profile of the critical success factors of partnerable consultative sellers:

- Gains rewards by rewarding others, credits others for their contributions, likes to mentor others and leave them improved.
- Negotiates by presenting options for the single best solution. Asks "What if?" rather than tells "What-to."
- Enjoys collaboration. Acts as coleader and comanager. Demonstrates acute people-sensitivity.
- Displays high frustration tolerance. Enters unstructured situations and shapes them according to the consultative model.
- Lives a consultative lifestyle. Partners at work or play.
- Stands up to being evaluated.

Customer satisfaction for clients is not a prescription from Dr. Feelgood. It is a pairing of two quantifiable outcomes that come together to form the standards of minimally satisfactory partner performance:

- *Zero cost,* which requires that all significant discretionary expenditures must be investments, not costs, and as such they must earn a positive return.
- *Zero risk,* which requires 100 percent certainty of achieving each proposed profit improvement.

These are the "hurdle rates" for satisfying clients. That means they get you in the door, but they do not compel a customer to invite you to sit down and partner. They serve to put a floor under your performance. You provide the ceiling, consisting of the height of the profits you can contribute and the frequency rate with which you can repeat your contributions. These are the measurements that determine how high your customers' satisfaction with you can be.

Departnering occurs when two conditions are met. An alliance that is incomplete or unfulfilled within itself is vulnerable. When a more promising partner appears, it succumbs. Many troubled partnerships linger on because both partners temporarily subscribe to the belief that "You know what you've got, but you don't know what you're going to get." As soon as one partner believes that what he or she is going to get is better, the partnership will end. In Consultative Selling, this means that the client will also be lost.

Because markets are tight communities, the loss of one client inevitably raises doubts, creates assumptions, and fosters anxieties that threaten the stability of other client relations. A domino effect can follow. The loss of one key account opens the door to competitors who, even if they have not been a cause of departnering, will be anxious to take advantage of its effects.

What leaves a partnership incomplete or causes it to be unfulfilled? There are two major factors that predispose to eventual departnering: divergence of objective and inequality of risk.

1. *Divergent objective.* Partnerships rest on a common objective. Both partners must have the same result in mind before they partner, see the same result as being achieved while they are partnering, and be able to look back at the accomplishment of their result as a consequence of the partnership.

Consultative partnerships are known by the objective the partners have in common. The eternal question of what partners see in each other is easily answered: They want to achieve the same objective, and they perceive the partnership as the optimal means of reaching it. This is their hidden agenda.

A consultative partnership is not a one-on-one situation. More accurately, it is a two-for-one relationship. Both partners share one objective—to improve the client's profit. Unless this is accomplished, the consultant's objective of improving profit on sales will be impossible. For this reason, the client's objective must come first for both of them. It is not philanthropy but enlightened self-interest that makes it so.

When objectives diverge, or simply appear to be going off in different directions or losing conviction, alliances atomize. A client partner may acquire the belief that the consultant is more interested in self-promotion to the client's top tier than in merchandising the partnership. The client partner may feel used, demeaned, and taken unfair advantage of by helping the consultant develop business elsewhere, either inside or outside the organization. The consultant, on the other hand, may believe many of the same things about the client partner. Whether such perceptions are true or not, they will have an erosive effect on the partnership.

Restating objectives and recommitting to them are essential elements in keeping partnerships on track. Objectives should be brought up for discussion at frequent intervals; this should be at the consultant's initiative. A good time to introduce them is when progress is being measured against them. At some of these checkpoints, the original objective may have to be downgraded. Perhaps it can be increased. In either event, keeping objectives current perpetuates the values that both partners are working for.

2. *Unequal risk.* Partnerships are a means of reducing risk. Two parties can share the load, divide the responsibility, and parcel out the components of the risk that would otherwise be borne by one or left undone. Although risk can be reduced, it can never be eliminated. It must be shared as equally as possible if the partnership is to be preserved. Otherwise, one partner may accuse the other of "putting your hand out further than your neck."

No matter how hard consultants try to bring into balance the risks inherent in improving customer profits, clients will always be left with the major exposure. They are exposed on their own behalf. They are exposed on their recommendation of the consultant. And they are exposed to their topmost tier of management. In any business situation, there can be no riskier combination of exposures.

Once clients commit themselves to work with a consultant to

improve their profit, they must be successful. It is no wonder that they will be ultrasensitive to their own inherent risk and to the support they receive from you.

There is no way you can have the same degree of risk as your clients incur, but you can provide a greater degree of risk calculation and limitation. This must be your equalizer.

OBSESSING ON CONTROL

The Box Two mindset is obsessed with *control*. Every manager knows that costs must be controlled. So must sales, since too much demand that cannot be met can overwhelm manufacturing, inventory, and distribution just as seriously as too little demand can underwhelm them. If shipments get out of control, managers get into trouble. An uncontrolled rate of scrap or mean-time between downtime or repair and replacement under warranty, or market share that deviates from plan, is an ominous sign that managers are going to be off budget and off plan. This will bring them to the attention of Box One.

In most customer companies, deviations from plan call for Box One to "manage by exception"—to apply supervisory management practices and procedures to correct the exceptions and either get the manager back on plan or find a new manager who will be unexceptional. Box One's philosophy is often expressed like this: "When managers go off plan, I invite them to lunch. No one gets invited to lunch twice."

When customer managers partner with you, their purpose is to reduce the risk of being invited to a "box lunch" by Box One. That is why you must be sure that you can help them achieve the new contributions to profits, either by cost reductions or revenue increases, that you have proposed to them and that they can achieve them within the time you propose. Otherwise you will expose them to catastrophic risk.

To be "in control" means that a manager is on plan—on budget, on time, attaining each milestone on schedule—so that payback of Box One's investment can be made on or before its due date and so that the manager's return on investment reaches its projected rate. This is the way that your Box Two partners build their track record as good managers. As good managers, they will again be favored to manage the next cycle of investment, and you will again be favored to be their partner in replicating your mutual success. Together, you will become a reliable team.

All business is based on reliability. Customers prize reliability over every other attribute—in their people, their products and services, their operations, and their reputations for their own customers' satisfaction. To be out of control is to be unreliable, which means that the profit contribution you and your partner have proposed cannot be *counted on* any longer. You should take these words literally. The expression "counted on" is a quantitative measure of your value, and it says very clearly that you and your customer-partner will come in with new profits as scheduled or you and your partner may be out.

Making PIPs that can be counted on is your transcendent task. It is the basis for your partnered positioning. Take that away, and you have what the computer industry calls *vaporware* and the food industry calls *empty calories*—promise without performance, the essence of unreliability.

In order to be an acceptable partner for customers' Box Two managers, you must share their obsession with control. In consultative terms, control means two things: controlling clients' costs to help them maintain low-cost production, and controlling the flow of their revenues to help them maintain high margins or high market share.

To be admitted into a major client partnership depends on a single compelling requirement: Can you bring more money to the client's party than any other candidate for partnership?

If you "make partner," you can achieve control of the contributions to costs, revenues, and earnings in the clients' business functions and lines of business that you affect. They will place responsibility for controlling these contributions in your hands, either as a dedicated supplier or as a facility manager of their operations. As their partner, they will count on you—counting dollar by dollar, in the most literal sense—to deliver your contributions "on the money" and on time.

By controlling your contributions according to the proposals you make to your clients, you control the continuity of your business with them. If your contributions slow or falter, your partnerships will be in trouble. Every time you deliver a proposed contribution, you earn the right to propose again. If you lose control of your ability to improve a client's profits dependably, you will lose your client.

So what is it that you can actually control? It is not the client, nor is it the client's business. You can control only the contributions you make to it.

As a result, PIP control becomes essential for partnering. Your PIPs must be reliable contributors to customer profits. The best way to ensure this is to set up a three-phase process of PIP control:

1. *PIP previews.* These enable each client-consultant team to preview the potential proposals in each account's fast-penetration plan, rank them in priority order of their perceived sureness in dollar value and timeliness, and then certify their value before presentation.

2. *PIP reviews.* These enable each team to review each proposal after its acceptance to warrant its deliverability and to schedule its monitoring and measurement milestones to make certain that its full proposed value is progressively delivered.

3. *PIP overviews.* These enable each team to agree on each PIP's contribution, to log it in their joint database, and to seek follow-on enhancements for it and natural migration opportunities in the near-term future. At each overview, the partnership's norms for improved customer profits can be updated to keep them current.

Accounts that get out of control are caused by PIP management processes that become uncontrollable. Through PIP management, you can always know where you stand in account control by asking questions like these:

- Are we making the profit contributions we are proposing?
- Are we measuring and monitoring them with our customers?

- Are we keeping up enough "PIP flow" to earn our partnership all over again every day?
- Are we maintaining our contributions above the level of the industry standard?
- Are we generating a steady state of future leads from each completed proposal?
- Are we making our competitors *beat us* in our norms or *beat it?*

PART II

PROPOSING CONTINUOUS BUSINESS IMPROVEMENT THROUGH FAST-CLOSING PROFIT PROJECTS

CONSULTATIVE PROPOSING STRATEGIES

7

How to Qualify Customer Problems

The high margins that accrue from Consultative Selling are your reward for knowing more about the customer operations you affect—and being able to improve them—than your competitors do. Margins are merited by mastery of how a customer runs the business lines and functions that are your sales targets. The more you know about them, and the better you are able to implement what you know into proposals for performing them more cost-effectively, the greater your value will be—accordingly, the higher the price you will deserve.

Consultative Selling is industry-specific. Within each industry, it is operation-specific. Business operations in customer companies are your end users, your true markets. According to the way they operate, they create the costs that you can reduce or do away with entirely. They can add new sales revenues or productivity if you can show them how. Your customer's business operations are the sources of the problems you have to solve and the showcases where the value of your solutions gives testimony to your capabilities. Scoping their ways of operating should therefore be your constant preoccupation.

If you are going to sell in a consultative manner, customer business operations will be the subject matter of your consultation. The only alternative is to talk about your own processes and the products or services they produce. In that case, you will be talking to the purchasing tier and selling on a basis of competitive performance and price. Your opportunity for high margins will have vanished.

DEVELOPING BUSINESS OPERATIONS PROFILES

All business operations have a flow—they have a beginning, a middle, and an end. Manufacturing begins with raw materials and ends with finished goods in inventory. Data processing begins with raw information and ends with reports. There are costs at both ends; in between, there is nothing but costs.

Consultative sales representatives should be able to chart the flow of the critical customer business operations they affect. They should be able to assign appropriate costs to the most critical success factors in each process—the 20 percent that contribute the 80 percent—and be able to prescribe the optimal remedy to reduce their contribution to costs or expand their contribution to revenues.

Some of these remedies will be therapeutic; that is, they will lower an existing cost. Other remedies will be curative; they will alter a process, combine it with another, or eliminate it from the flow. In still other cases, the remedy will be to change the architecture of a process so that a completely new set of cost or revenue centers will result.

In most customer operations, work flow is cost-ineffective. It incurs unnecessary cost or it processes work ineffectively. If you can optimize it, you can improve its contribution to profits. Every dollar of cost you take out can drop to the customer's bottom line. Every improvement you make in productivity can also lower the operating cost and raise the output from each dollar invested in labor, energy, and materials.

There are two ways to scope a customer business line or business function. One is to scope its funding to determine where it ranks in its company's flow of investment funds. A second way is to scope its process flow to determine its critical success factors.

1. *Scoping funding.* Nothing happens in business until funds flow. Once funds are allocated, they can be drawn down at the

Box Two level and put to work, that is, invested. If consultative sellers want work, they must go where the funds are flowing, which will always be to a customer's cost center and profit center managers whose success is critical to corporate strategy.

"Go where funds flow" prevents your coming up dry by being told, "We have no money," and having proposals turned back that are in effect stamped "insufficient funds."

2. *Scoping process.* When funds flow to a profit-centered line of business or cost center, work can flow through it. You must know how this takes place. You must be able to identify the critical success factors in all customer functions that you affect, you must know their current contributions to function costs or revenues, and you must know if you can add value to them and at what rate of return for a customer's investment.

Figure 7-1 shows the critical functions that determine the success of a supermarket chain's business. Where are costs higher than necessary: Is inventory stocking or order assembly inefficient? Where are revenue opportunities remaining undercapitalized: Can backhaul trucking be made to contribute, or contribute more, to profits?

The work flow for an aerospace manufacturer is shown in Figure 7-2. This process begins with the marketing function. How can it turn over more projects faster? Are design analysis and testing roadblocks to turning over the process as a whole? Is time wasted, and therefore money, in moving along the projects that marketing brings in? What if model testing could be accomplished one month faster? One week faster? What value would that add to delivery, the time when an aerospace manufacturer is paid in full? In other words, what would the added value be of reducing the cycle time of receivables collection by one month for each project?

All PIPs prescribe a solution for work flow problems or cycle time problems or sometimes for both. A PIP can propose to reduce the number of work stations in a process or re-engineer the way they operate or how they are organized. Other PIPs can propose to reduce the time required for a workstation to complete its op-

Figure 7-1. Supermarket chain work flow.

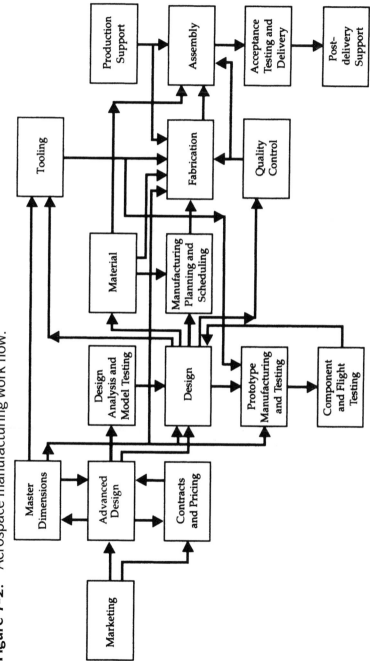

Figure 7-2. Aerospace manufacturing work flow.

erating cycle, speeding up work flow but leaving essentially unchanged the way the process is engineered.

Whenever you PIP customers' cycle time, such as getting a new product to market faster or shipping more orders the same day or turning over collections quicker, you are affecting the time value of money in addition to its volume. All of these improvements bring in money faster. In some cases, they may bring in more money than if the customers were to come late to a market or lose one of their key customers to a competitor because of the inability to fill an order when it is received.

In other cases, where your customers would have made the same amount of money anyway, you can PIP only its time value. This may occur in the form of a short-term margin advantage or faster interest accrual from putting the money to work sooner.

In a PIP opportunity where time values are of major importance, a "what-if?" would be expressed like this:

"What if we can help you get each new model to market 30 days faster? This can increase your profits by an average $100,000 per model, based on an incremental month's supply of first-mover margins that earn an average 20 percent premium. When you multiply $100,000 by twelve new models per year, the total improved profit comes to $1.2 million. To realize it, you need to invest only $330,000, which is paid back within the first half year."

DATABASING FROM CUSTOMER SOURCES

To vend, you need to know your own costs. To sell in a consultative manner, you need to know customer costs. To vend, you need to know your own sales opportunities. To sell as a consultant, you need to know customer sales opportunities. Realizing that you must come up with a cost-reducing or revenue-adding option, how can you learn a customer's current costs in the business functions that are important to you? How can you get a fix on the customer's unachieved sales potential? In profiling customer operations, how can you quantify with reasonable accuracy the problems and opportunities that will form the base of your penetration plans?

You need to develop three databases, storehouses of information that become the basic resources for value-based selling to key accounts:

1. An *industry database* on each of the industries in which you serve key customers
2. A *customer database* on each key account customer you serve in an industry
3. A *customer's customer database* on your key accounts' key accounts

From your industry database, you learn average costs, average profits on sales, average inventories and receivables, and other industry norms. The information in each of your key customer databases allows you to compare customer performance against industry averages. In categories where a customer falls below the norms, you may find sales opportunities.

Your individual customer databases teach you the concentration and distribution of customer costs. Where do they bunch up? Are these the same places for the industry as a whole? How heavy are they? What are their trends? Are they rising or are they coming under control? What variable factors affect them most significantly?

The best answers to all of these questions always come from customers themselves. Supplementary and complementary data can be found in public information sources listed in Figure 7-3.

Your customer databases also provide you with knowledge of where potential new sales opportunities for a customer may be found. These may include existing products, new products, combined products, new or enhanced services, superproducts, or systems. How can your customers sell more? How can they sell at higher prices? How can they extend sales into closely adjacent markets? How can they invade new markets that offer superior profit opportunity? How can they anticipate or turn back a competitive thrust?

In order for you to know your customers' businesses, you must know more than the performance and cost characteristics of the internal business functions that you can affect. You must also know the markets your customers sell to. They are your custom-

Figure 7-3. Public information sources.

Customer Information

- Quarterly, annual, and 10-K reports
- Investment analyst research reports
- *Standard & Poor's Corporate Records*
- *Standard & Poor's Register of Corporations*
- *Standard & Poor's Industrial Surveys*
- *Thomas Register of American Manufacturers*
- *Ward's Business Directory*
- *Dun & Bradstreet Reports*
- *Value Line Investment Surveys*
- Compustat database on public companies
- Internet *Alta Vista Document Search*
- AOL/America Online *Hoover's Business Sources*
- *Lexis/Nexis* Online
- *U.S. Department of Commerce U.S. Industrial Outlook*

Financial Ratios

- *Prentice-Hall's Almanac of Business and Industrial Financial Ratios*
- *Dun & Bradstreet Industry Norms and Key Business Ratios*
- *Standard & Poor's Analyst's Handbook*
- *Robert Morris Associates Annual Statement Study of Financial and Operating Ratios*

ers' opportunity. Their needs cause many customer business functions to operate the way they do: to manufacture the kinds of products they make, to advertise and sell the way they do, to communicate inside and outside their businesses with the telecommunications and data processing technologies they use. Only when you know your customers' customers can you understand the full range of sales opportunities that can be enlarged as well as costs that can be reduced.

The essential elements of information you need to know about your customers' customers are exactly the same as the data

you must develop on your customers themselves. You have to learn the major cost areas your customers affect in their own key account businesses and the main sales opportunities they help them achieve.

When you have accumulated your databases, make sure that you know the five "must knows" in order to PIP most cost-effectively:

From All Operating Managers

1. What are the best of breeds (BOBs) in your operation and how do you compare to competition?
2. What are the under-the-gun KPIs for your operation right now and how much/how soon must you improve them?

From Line-of-Business Managers

3. What are the critical success factors (CSFs) in your operation?
4. What is the economic value added (EVA) by each one percent improvement in:
   - Share point?
   - Same-day shipments?
   - Reduction in on-hand inventory?
   - Improvement in margins?
   - Reduction in cost of sales?

From Business Function Managers

5. What is the economic value added by each one percent improvement in:
   - Downtime?
   - Scrap?
   - Labor intensity?
   - Product development cycle?
   - Billing-collection cycle time?

The five "must knows" represent the crucial data points for PIPping. The only place you can learn them is from the managers

of the customer operations whose contributions to profits you want to improve.

• Knowing the functions and processes that are best of breed tells you where a manager will allocate priority funds to maintain leadership. Where a manager's operation is not best of breed in a critical success factor tells you that funds must be allocated to gain or regain competitive advantage.

• Knowing the factors that are critical to an operation's success tells you where to prospect for closable leads whose problems must be solved fast and whose opportunities must be seized before a market changes or a competitor gets there first.

• Knowing the economic value that can be added to a line-of-business or a supportive business function by various strategies tells you where you can propose the most closable PIPs and gives you a dollarized baseline for calculating an incremental improvement by following the principle of the power of one—in this case, one percent. Even a one percent improvement in the contribution added by a current strategy that yields a high value can be significant.

In order to induce customer managers to share their numbers with you, there is one immutable rule to follow: *To get customer numbers, you must offer your own numbers first.* The numbers you offer must be the best projection of your norms onto your best estimate of a customer's current performance.

Being sure of your solution means more than just being sure that it will work. Does it yield the best financial reward—in other words, do the dollar values work best? If you are wrong, millions of dollars may be sacrificed, as one customer discovered:

We make hundreds of components that can be configured in thousands of ways to make an unlimited number of customized products. One vendor wanted to set up a just-in-time inventory of all our components. Another one gave us a system to determine the optimal configuration for each product based on customer require-

ments. The JIT inventory would have saved us between $3 and $5 million. But the second vendor saved us roughly $18 to $20 million per year in manufacturing costs by reducing the number of false orders for unneeded components.

Proposing the Power of One

The number one, which is the smallest whole number, can have enormous power. One more product sold every day, one more percentage point added to current revenues or profits every week, or one more day gained every month in the collection of accounts receivable can yield astonishing amounts of improved profits for a customer. Applying the power of one also appeals to customer comfort. Most managers can deal with increments of that magnitude without incurring a disruption of the business whose costs and inefficiencies can nullify the gains. Furthermore, the number one has the power of credibility. Most customers will readily concede that they can improve performance, productivity, or profits by 1 percent.

The power of one is the basis of PIP power. It is your power base for a customer's profit improvement. If the power of one is powerful enough, it may also be your end point. If you propose to increase an inventory manager's turnover cycle, you need to know the power of improving the number of turns by one a year. If your customer were IBM, with a $10 billion inventory that was turning over 2.8 times a year, each additional turn can save $2 billion in cash that no longer needs to be tied up financing unsold computers. If you propose to decrease an airline manager's operating costs, you need to know the power of reducing costs by each cent. If your customer were Delta, each 1 cent reduction in the cost of flying one seat one mile can earn the equivalent of $600 million a year in new revenues.

The power of one applies equally across the board of customer operations, as the following examples show for information systems:

- If an airline's reservation system goes down for one hour, it can cost a minimum of $1 million in lost sales.
- If a manufacturer's mission-critical network goes down for one hour, it can cost an average of $100,000 in delayed transactions.
- If a Wall Street brokerage's distribution system goes down for one hour, it can cost up to $100 million in lost stock and bond purchases.

When the power of one is applied to reducing inventory overstock by 1 percent, three sources of added value can be created:

1. Interest cost on capital invested in inventory can be reduced.
2. Carrying charges for slow-moving and stationary items in inventory can be saved, often subtracting up to 25 percent of total inventory contribution to distribution costs.
3. Write-offs for obsolete products can be scaled back.

Even more sources of added value can be created by reducing inventory out-of-stock by 1 percent:

1. Same-day order fulfillment and just-in-time deliveries can be increased, keeping billings and collections current.
2. Production downtime from lack of parts can be reduced, along with machine take-down and set-up costs to manufacture small makeup runs.
3. High turnover of the highest profit-contributing products can be ensured, especially important when 1 percent of all products accounts for a disproportionately large percent of receivables.
4. Lost orders and lost customers can be minimized.

For each of these examples, the Consultative Selling opening questions are the same:

"What if we start to reduce downtime one hour at a time? What is the smallest number of hours that can make a significant difference in revenues? What is their dollar value? If one hour is

significant, as in the Wall Street brokerage example, what if we start with that?"

Multiple-Sourcing the Power of One

The power of one's value can come from multiple sources. By reducing inventory overstocking by one percent, the value can come from a combination of reduced interest cost on the capital invested in inventory, reduced carrying charges for slow-moving and stationary items that together can add up to 25 percent or more of total inventory contribution to distribution costs, and reduced write-off for obsolete products.

What if the customer's inventory problem is being out of stock, and you can reduce it by 1 percent? The value can come from several sources:

- Higher turnover of the highest profit-contributing products that yield more than 80 percent of annual revenues.
- Accelerated billing and collection cycle from increased same-day order fulfillment.
- Reduced lost orders, reduced lost customers, and increased customer satisfaction.
- Reduced take-down and set-up manufacturing costs for small make-up runs.

The power of one can show up in the added purchasing power of one new customer for your own customer. If you find yourself proposing that your own customer should invest $1 million with you in new equipment, stop before you go any further and ask what you should be consultatively persuading him to buy. It must not be the equipment. What the customer is buying is an extra $1 million in annual sales at a contribution margin of $250,000 that is enabled by the enlarged capacity the equipment can provide. Before you can propose, you must know two things:

1. One million dollars worth of incremental annual demand exists.
2. The return on the customers' investment compensates

them for the incremental cost at or above their hurdle rate. This means that you must know that the customers' 25 percent marginal return exceeds their minimum acceptable return of 20 percent on investments of $1 million.

If the demand exists and the investment's return is minimally acceptable, then all it may take to close a PIP is the annual income from one additional customer. This one customer's business is what you are actually proposing.

If General Valve Company sells its Twin Seals at $100,000 and a competitor comes in at $70,000, General must try to justify the extra $30,000. If it is not selling consultatively, it will vend the features and benefits of Twin Seals and end up discounting their value. But with Consultative Selling, General can earn more than its originally proposed $100,000.

When General sells to a petrochemicals refiner, its account managers go looking for leaking valves. When they find a valve that is leaking contaminants into a premium fuel facility, they have a closeable proposal opportunity. The refiner's potential loss on premium fuel that has been downgraded into regular fuel is $.03 per gallon. This can add up to an annual loss of $75,000 in each of the refiner's ten 2.52 million–gallon tanks for a total loss of $750,000 a year, year after year. Capturing this money converts a performance-to-price ratio to investment-to-return, making $100,000 irrelevant against the added value of $750,000 to infinity. If payback of the customer's investment can occur within twelve months, the investment becomes the equivalent of a short-term loan at the ROI's rate of interest.

General's account managers do not have to wait to discover leaks in a refiner's processes. They can anticipate their negative contributions to maintenance cost and revenues according to their norms. Ball valves and gate valves are always cheaper than General's Twin Seals. On initial purchase price alone they would win. But their costs of ownership can be prohibitive. If one of them leaks only 0.01 percent of a pipeline's total throughput, 28.8 barrels of marketable product will be lost. This amounts to 10.5 thousand barrels lost per valve per year. At an average product price of $10 a barrel, the annual cost of a ball valve or gate valve is actually over $100,000. When the price of oil rises, the valve's cost of ownership goes up with it. Refiners who deprive themselves of the benefits of Twin Seals can be shown to end up constructively "buying" them over and over again without ever enjoying their contributions to improved profits.

Codifying the Power of One

Some consultative sellers have codified the power of one in their businesses. For every 1 percent of cost reduction we can help a customer achieve, such a business can say, we can propose a 5 percent improvement in customer profits. For every 1 percent of added sales revenues we can bring to a customer, we can propose a 4 percent improvement in customer profits. For every 1 percent of added margin we can help a customer command, we can propose a 9 percent improvement in customer profits.

If you can help a manufacturing customer eliminate one part from a major product, you can free the business from ten contributions to cost. The customer will not have to:

1. Design it.
2. Assign a part number to it.
3. Inventory it.
4. Shelve it.
5. Inspect it.
6. Assemble it.
7. Repair it.
8. Package it.
9. Handle it.
10. Deliver it.

If you partner with customers to help them expand sales, can you enlarge their market opportunity by a factor of one? If you can start new mothers using a customer's baby foods one month sooner, when their babies are five months old instead of six, you can open your customer to millions of dollars worth of incremental annual sales.

Figures 7-4 and 7-5 are laundry lists of general opportunities

Figure 7-4. Revenue expansion opportunities.

1. Add operational flexibility.
2. Add manufacturing or processing quality.
3. Add volume.
4. Improve effectiveness of sales department.
5. Introduce new sizes, shapes, or materials or new and improved products.
6. Reduce customer returns.
7. Apply creative sales promotion strategies.
8. Speed up production and distribution.
9. Reduce or eliminate unprofitable products, customers, warehouses, or territories.
10. Improve market position.
11. Add brand name value.
12. Add customer benefits.
13. Extend product life.
14. Expand into new markets.
15. Increase distribution.

Figure 7-5. Cost reduction opportunities.

1. Reduce number of operations.
2. Reduce cost of one or more operations.
3. Combine two or more operations.
4. Automate operations.
5. Reduce labor.
6. Improve production scheduling.
7. Reduce operating time to speed up production.
8. Reduce insurance costs.
9. Reduce materials consumption.
10. Recycle materials.
11. Substitute less expensive materials or otherwise reformulate product.
12. Reduce raw materials inventory.
13. Reduce parts inventory.
14. Improve controls.
15. Simplify product and package design.

to apply the power of one to revenue expansion and cost reduction. Somewhere in these lists may be your own best opportunities, the things you do exceptionally well that help customers improve their profits and that therefore become the definition of "what you do" as a business. These elements of "your game" target the critical success factors in customer businesses and business functions that identify the arenas where you can make the partnership contributions that must become your industry's standards for adding value.

The world of costs is changing. Whereas labor has traditionally contributed the major share of a manufacturer's costs, now it rarely exceeds 10 to 20 percent. While the hard-core costs of capital equipment have traditionally been a principal area of customer investment, or at least have been perceived as such, this is no longer the case in businesses in which information-intensive services are natural accompaniments of equipment. In buying computers, for example, a common rule of thumb is to allow $100 for training expenses for every $1 of hardware cost. In networking computers and telecommunications equipment, the support costs of making everything work together as a single coherent system normally outruns the equipment cost by five times. These customer costs for integration and application are more important to reduce, in many cases, than are the costs of the hard goods they add to.

GETTING TO **PIP**

Nothing happens in Consultative Selling until you get to PIP. At the PIP point, you make your preliminary PIP to customer managers and begin your partnership. This begins the process of putting you in business with them. It positions you as potentially partnerable, permitting the belief that you may provide them with a compelling reason to work with you. At the same time that a preliminary PIP starts the selling phase of the sales cycle, it also forecloses to your competition the customer problem or opportunity you have projected for improvement.

The sooner you can get to PIP, the better. Until you do, you are vulnerable to opportunity cost from not being able to sell. You are also open to preemption by a competitor who can get to PIP faster or by the closing of the opportunity window if customer priorities change, managers change jobs or their positions become consolidated, or funds run out or become reallocated. Simultaneously, your customers are also suffering lost opportunity and may be preempted in industry advantage by their own competitors.

When you sell improved profits, time becomes your enemy. Time downgrades the value of money, which has a time value as well as a dollar value. The rule of thumb about money is that a dollar today is always worth more than the value of the same dollar tomorrow because today's dollar can be invested today to make more dollars. Tomorrow's dollar must wait for tomorrow. This is as true for your business as it is for your customer. The longer it takes you to get to PIP, the less money you make and the more money you spend in cost of sales to make it.

Customer managers are in business to do deals. A deal is an investment that yields positive return. Profit Improvement Proposals are invitations to deal by making an investment in an application of your products, services, or systems to improve customer profits.

From a customer's perspective, there are six major hurdles that your PIPs must clear in order to be considered a good deal:

1. The *expected return,* expressed by the customer's question, "How much do I get out of it?" There are two ways of proposing your answer. One is the cash flow from year-one expanded revenues or reduced costs. The other is the net present value of all future cash flows beyond the first year discounted back to the present and calculated over the productive life of the investment.

2. The *proposed investment,* expressed by the customer's question, "How much do I have to put in?"

3. The *internal rate of return,* expressed by the customer's question, "What is the ratio between how much I get out of it and how much I have to put in?" The answer is the annual percentage return per dollar invested.

4. The *payback,* expressed by the customer's question, "How soon do I recover my investment?"

5. The *opportunity cost,* expressed by the customer's question, "How much do I lose by saying no?" The answer is the total net positive cash flow payout over the productive life of the investment.

6. The *earliest point at which risk can be controlled,* expressed by the customer's question, "If I don't like it once I'm into it, how soon can I get out?" The answer is the first checkpoint at which results are measured.

A PIP becomes closable because it is more advantageous for customers to live with your solution than to go on living with their current problem or inability to take advantage of an opportunity.

Closable PIPs are delivery vehicles for "killer apps"—applications of a supplier's technology to a customer's operation that maximize improved profits. A killer app kills off a problem or kills off competitive proposals to realize the same opportunity. It kills off procrastination because, operationally and financially, its results are compelling. When a killer app is first proposed, it stops debate dead in its tracks. Its top-line and bottom-line contributions make customers want to get their hands on them. The new profits seem realizable. The operating improvements that enable them seem achievable. Delay seems unjustifiable.

At first sight, many killer apps appear to be no-brainers. Quite the opposite. They come out of a consultative seller's grey matter: the ability to reach into his or her database on customer operations along with their needs and objectives, and especially their current contributions to revenues and costs, coupled with the knowledge of how supplier technology can best be applied to affect them. This ability to mix and match reveals the "matrix mind" of the consultative seller. In a continuous filtering manner, the seller is screening customer operating norms through the templates of supplier improvement norms. Killer apps come into being when the two intersect.

Your PIPs must radiate credibility in the advantages they propose. They start out with one strike against them. Every customer manager knows about—or even worse, has lived through—the $250,000 investment that grew to $500,000 in order to save a $1 million return that was promised to be twice as much but shrank to less than half by the time it was realized.

Every manager's common experience also includes the six-month payback that stretched out to sixteen. There are three ways to make your PIPs credible. One is to make all your preliminary calculations on the conservative side, leaving yourself "wiggle room" when you work with your customer's numbers:

- Overestimate all costs by 20 percent.
- Underestimate all revenues by 20 percent.

The second way is to promise a small number of benefits. It is easier to achieve the correction of a customer's parts shortage all by itself than to combine it with improving productivity, enhancing customer service, and speeding up inventory turns all in the same PIP. The third way is to work with your customer's numbers. If you propose to reduce customers' inventories, start with their current cost of goods sold—for example, $3 million. Then put their numbers to work like this:

- A customer values their current inventory at $800,000.
- The current turn rate is therefore 3.75, the result of dividing the cost of goods sold by the inventory value.
- If you propose to reduce inventory by 10 percent, or $80,000, leaving an inventory value of $720,000, the improved inventory turn rate is 4.16.
- If the customer agrees that the cost of carrying $80,000 worth of inventory is 25 percent (to account for handling, insurance, shrinkage, damage, space, obsolescence, taxes, and the opportunity cost of tied-up cash), the total savings come to $20,000.

The customer will buy this number because customer numbers have gone into it.

If customer business improvement is to be continuous, PIP-ping must also be continuous. The key to seizing competitive advantage as a profit improver is the ability to make fast incremental improvements in customer profits. This requires a fast-cycle PIP capability.

Some PIPs are the result of an unanticipated customer demand. Most PIPs come from a consultative seller's initiative to solve a proposable opportunity.

PIP opportunities are sourced by the seller's use of norms to target a mismatch between a norm and a customer's current performance. An opportunity is triggered whenever the seller's norm can make the customer more advantaged.

When consultative sellers compete against each other, the edge goes to the faster cycler of closable PIPs. It must be assumed that all consultative sellers have equal access to customer information and are equipped with technologies that are at par. Applications skill remains your sole proprietary asset. It allows you to come up with a more closable solution in spite of implementing a similar technology to solve the same customer problem or opportunity. But "time to PIP" is a qualifier of applications skill.

Even a superior outcome based on superior applications skill loses its time value unless it can be fast-cycled. Not only does PIP-speed expand the likelihood of customer preference in the face of alternative choices, it also can collapse a competitor's ability to respond. When this occurs, your credibility for being reliable—to your competitor's detriment—is enhanced.

PIPping in the "Red Zone"

If you are going to have a norm of 1:1 for PIPs closed to PIPs proposed, you must get into the customer managers' "red zone," where they are compelled to take action on each PIP you present. It is not enough to say that your proposal "certainly made them sit up and take notice" or that the outcome of your presentation was that you made them think. A thinking manager is not a closing manager. Your outcome must be to get a close. What will get you into the red zone where you can score?

Customer managers' red zones are where their key performance indicators (KPIs) are located. Each PIP must fit one of them in order to link it to the manager's contribution to business strategy. This is called a PIP's business fit. A statement of business fit sounds like this:

This proposal contributes to realizing your business objectives to:

1. Increase your sales volume by $4.5 million (42.4 percent) over the next three years.
2. Increase your market share by 4.1 points (10 percent).
3. Increase your net operating profits before tax (NOPBT) by $2.3 million (9 percent).

In the course of your partnering, you will learn each customer's business objectives. Your PIPs must tie their contributions to these objectives by quantifying how much of each objective you can help realize: for example, contributing $864,000 (4 percent) toward the customer's sales volume objective of $4.5 million and increasing NOPBT by $69,000 per year to contribute 30 percent of the operating profit objective.

KPIs compose a customer manager's "plan." The manager's current performance is called "actual." If plan exceeds actual, the manager is "off plan" and at risk of becoming competitively disadvantaged. Disadvantages can become your leads if your norms represent an improvement over a customer's actual performance when it is below a KPI.

The performance indicators that you choose to improve for your customers provide them with their definition of your business. The KPIs you decide to "own" position you with customer managers in terms of exactly *where* in their operations you can partner with them and *why,* because of your norms, they are compelled to partner with you. The "where" is your entry point.

If you want to make yourself compelling to IT managers, for example, nothing will do it faster or on a more businesslike basis than to issue norm challenges like these:

- Do your operating costs exceed our norm of 1 percent of the dollar value of all the purchases you make? If so, what if we can work together to bring you closer to our norm?
- Does your staff exceed our norm of 2.2 per each $100 million to $150 million worth of purchases?

- Does your number of instances of delayed shipments exceed our norm of four to six total yearly deliveries from each supplier?

If you want to compel hospital managers to do business with you, challenge them with your norms for their KPIs for capacity utilization expressed in terms of patient occupancy rate and average length of stay for patients in each disease category. You can also challenge other KPIs for the percent of outpatient revenues to total revenues, gross revenues per discharged patient, cash flow per bed, and the percent of salary and benefits expenses of hospital employees to the hospital's total expenses. Comparing labor costs to total costs shows how well a hospital is controlling its workforce content. Cash flow per bed shows how aggressively the hospital is recruiting patients, and their average length of stay shows how well the hospital is managing its turnover. If your norm for labor costs is 51 percent of total costs while hospital managers can do no better than 56.6 percent, you have a lead for a PIP to improve their performance.

If you sell IV systems for intravenous drug delivery to health care organizations as IFLOW does, you may need to know the key performance indicators of more than one class of customer manager. In IFLOW's case, critical care and neonatal unit heads are major users, as are general service IV team leaders. Pharmacy managers are involved as well, in addition to hospital administrators and their chief financial officers. In IFLOW's initial incarnation as a vendor, the critical success factors influencing sales were competitive price and performance, salesperson skills, timing, and supplier reputation. After reincarnation as a consultative seller, the chief factor critical to IFLOW's sales success has become the contribution that it can make to key users' KPIs.

At the Box One HMO and hospital administrator level and at the Box Two midlevels, there are several performance indicators to choose for improvement:

- Capacity utilization, such as the number of beds in service, occupancy rate, and average length of stay, all of which IFLOW can affect

151

- Revenues and expenses, such as cash flow per bed, total profit margin, and return on assets
- Productivity and efficiency, such as the ratio of personnel per patient and total assets turnover, as well as outcomes in terms of patient discharges in compliance with disease-category standards for length of stay

LEAD TARGETING WITH KPI NORMS

Key performance indicators come in two types:

1. Dollar values, expressed as minimum revenue or maximum cost objectives
2. Ratios, expressed as percentages

Some KPI classifications are standard across all industries. They are part of a manager's position title. Other KPIs are industry-specific.

KPIs for Profit Center Managers

Position title predicts the key indicators for all profit center managers' performances. They are evaluated by financial and working capital indicators of line-of-business performance such as:

- Total revenues, which are total receipts from sales
- Total operating income, which is gross profits minus total operating expenses
- Total operating expenses, which are costs of sales plus G&A plus R&D
- Cost of goods sold, which is sales compensation plus sales support and sales training
- Inventory turnover, which is the ratio of annual net sales compared to end-of-year inventory
- Accounts receivable turnover, which is the ratio of annual net sales compared to average receivables outstanding

Profit center managers are also evaluated by how well they handle key indicators of their operating performance:

- Gross profit, which is total revenues minus cost of goods sold
- Net profit, which is after-tax net income minus net sales
- Productivity, which is sales revenue minus cost of labor
- Selling efficiency, which is expressed in several ratios that compare sales revenues against selling expense, finished goods inventory, order backlog, same-day order fulfillment, and accounts receivable

If your customers manage a soft drink bottler, any significant deviations between the key indicators of their performance and your norms for them can become a proposable lead:

- How much of their capacity are they utilizing?
- How many cases per employee are they shipping?
- How much of their run time is interrupted by downtime?
- How much gross margin are they earning per case?
- How much of their sales revenue is held up in accounts receivable?
- How much of their customer base are they satisfying?

KPIs for Cost Center Managers

Cost center managers have function-specific KPIs:

- If they manage R&D, they are evaluated—among other indicators—by a ratio comparing the number of products developed to the number of products commercialized.
- If they manage manufacturing, they are evaluated by a ratio comparing the number of hours downtime to the number of hours uptime.
- If they manage inventory, they are evaluated by a ratio comparing the number of orders shipped the same day to the number of orders received.

Once you know what your customer managers are held to perform, you can propose to help them by targeting any indications that their actual performance lags your norm for their performance in categories like these:

Lead Targeting from Key Financial Performance Indicators. A customer's current financial performance can indicate opportunities for three kinds of profit improvement projects:

1. *Total Revenue Raisers.* You can propose to raise total revenues by speeding up time to market, increasing the turnover rate of the new product development cycle, improving forecasts or reducing inventory, adding distribution, or accelerating the billing and collection cycle.
2. *Total Operating Income Raisers.* You can propose to raise total operating income by increasing sales or decreasing operating expenses for cost of sales, G&A, and R&D.
3. *Cost of Goods Sold Reducers.* You can propose to reduce cost of goods sold by improving sales force productivity, reducing the sales cycle, adding distribution, opening up new sources of demand, or re-engineering sales strategy.

Lead Targeting from Key Operating Performance Indicators. A customer's current operating performance can indicate opportunities for four kinds of profit improvement projects:

1. *Gross Profit Raisers.* You can propose to raise gross profit by increasing sales volume and expanding market share, speeding up the sales cycle, adding distribution, increasing the turnover rate of the new product development cycle, or reducing manufacturing costs.
2. *Net Profit Raisers.* You can propose to raise net profit by increasing margins or reducing the cost of sales.
3. *Productivity Raisers.* You can propose to raise productivity by reducing labor content, increasing automation, or improving workforce training.
4. *Selling Efficiency Raisers.* You can propose to raise selling efficiency by reducing cost of sales, finished goods inven-

tory or order backlog, or by increasing same-day order fulfillment and accounts receivable collections.

Lead Targeting from Key Working Capital Performance Indicators. A customer's current working capital performance can indicate opportunities for two kinds of profit improvement projects:

1. *Inventory Turnover Raisers.* You can propose to raise inventory turnover by reducing inventory or helping to turn it faster.
2. *Accounts Receivable Turnover Raisers.* You can propose to raise accounts receivable turnover by helping to collect receivables faster.

OBSERVING YELLOW FLAGS

Not all lead opportunities are created equal. Some have subtle contraindications. Others are booby-trapped. Still others may be genuine opportunities that, at the time they become qualified leads, are for one reason or another inopportune. Your success as a consultative seller is predicated as much on the opportunities you walk away from as the ones you pursue.

Yellow flags like the thirteen that follow can give you fair warning. But only your judgment can make the right decision to go or no-go.

1. An opportunity is on the borderline of your core capability or outside the norms of your killer app.
2. An opportunity involves a customer operation that features a major process whose functionality is unfamiliar to you.
3. An opportunity demands a disproportionate commitment of your time and attendant costs.
4. An opportunity requires the cooperation of several third-party suppliers who are outside your control or oversight.

155

5. An opportunity has the potential for a series of progressive revisions over the course of its life cycle.

6. An opportunity was scoped and virtually finalized by others before your participation.

7. An opportunity is unlikely to improve your norms even if its outcome is realized, or it may actually downgrade your norms.

8. An opportunity has been postponed once before by the current customer manager.

9. An opportunity does not have a natural migration chain for follow-on proposals.

10. An opportunity cannot be finalized within the likely term of office of the current customer manager.

11. An opportunity carries such significant political meaning for the customer that an unsuccessful outcome could catastrophically shut down your future opportunities.

12. The opportunity carries the threat of your technology becoming obsolescent or replicated competitively before the project can be finalized, imperiling your perceived value and diminishing your claim to gainsharing.

13. The opportunity cost of not being able to manage a higher-value or lower-risk alternative project is high.

Compensating factors may make any of these risks manageable. The customer may be an influential reference. Migration opportunities may be significant. Your core resources may be more fully utilized and your inventory of experience may be enhanced by new successes. There may be the chance to lock out a competitor.

Comparisons and risks and rewards like these are inherent in the PIP proposal process. Most of the time when you make a wrong decision, it will be because your disregarded a risk's yellow flag in spite of your better judgment. The major risks to sweat are those that are dependent on time. Not only is time a cost. It is the one cost that cannot be reclaimed.

In common with all processes, quality control can be applied to the PIP process by setting Six Sigma standards for near-perfect results in four aspects of profit improvement proposing:

1. Realizing a one-to-one ratio of closed PIPs to proposed PIPs.
2. Eliminating time-consuming and costly variances in the process by which PIPs are prepared and presented.
3. Reducing the number and frequency of defects in PIP diagnosis, prescription, and cost-benefit analysis.
4. Meeting customer expectations at the 100 percent level that each PIP's actual benefits will equal its proposed benefits in both their dollar values and time values.

The PIP process is a replica of the Six Sigma process. In both, a lead is targeted by comparing an operation's current results with norms for better or best practices. The problem or opportunity is diagnosed. An improvement is prescribed and implemented. Its results are measured. They become the baseline for the next improvement in the continuous quest to get to Six Sigma for suppliers' PIPping and their customers' operations.

8

HOW TO QUANTIFY PIP
SOLUTIONS

Customer profit improvement begins with knowledge of how customers make the profits that you are going to improve: how they make their money right now. This is the starting point for Consultative Selling. Unless Consultative Selling strategies can improve the profits a customer can make, the customer will not be a prospect for high-margin sales.

A customer makes money based on five principles:

1. Circulating capital
2. Turnover
3. Contribution margin
4. Return on investment (ROI)
5. Payback

APPLYING THE CIRCULATING CAPITAL PRINCIPLE

Profit is made by the circulation of business capital. Every business is founded on capital or funds that start in the form of cash. The objective of business is to make the initial cash grow into more cash. This is accomplished by circulating the capital, the initial cash, through three transfer points. Each transfer adds value:

1. The initial cash circulates first into *inventories*.
2. Then the inventories circulate into *receivables*.

3. The receivables finally circulate back into *cash*, completing one cycle.

This three-step process demonstrates the principle of circulating capital. Every business depends on it for its income.

Circulating capital is the current assets of a business. They go to work in profitmaking as soon as cash is invested in accumulating inventories. Every time raw materials are purchased or processed, inventories come into existence. Another name for production scheduling could really be *inventory conversion*. Manufacturing adds further to the value of inventories, and so do all the other processing functions of a business that transfer value from cash to product costs on a dollar-for-dollar basis.

Figure 8-1 shows the profitmaking process that occurs as capital funds circulate through a customer's business. At *A* the funds are in the form of cash. As the business operates, the funds change form. The initial cash is transferred into inventories as raw materials are purchased, labor is paid, and finished goods are manufactured and transported from plant to warehouse.

When sales occur at *B*, funds flow from inventories—the manufactured goods—into receivables. As they flow, the magnitude of the funds increases because inventories are valued at cost and receivables are valued at selling price. This increase represents the gross profit on sales. The greater the gross profit rate, the greater the increase in funds during each rotation of the capital circulation cycle.

At *C*, the funds earned by the collection of receivables flow back once again into cash. Before they do, they are reduced by the sales and administrative expenses that have been disbursed throughout the operating cycle.

At this point, one full cycle of capital circulation has been completed. It has resulted in an increase in the number of dollars in the circulating capital fund. This increase is the difference between gross profits and selling/administrative expenses. In other words, a profit is made when the circulating capital of the business turns over one cycle. The more cycles through which you can help turn your customer's circulating capital during an operating year, the greater the profit the customer can earn. This is the principle of *turnover*.

Figure 8-1. Profitmaking capital circulation.

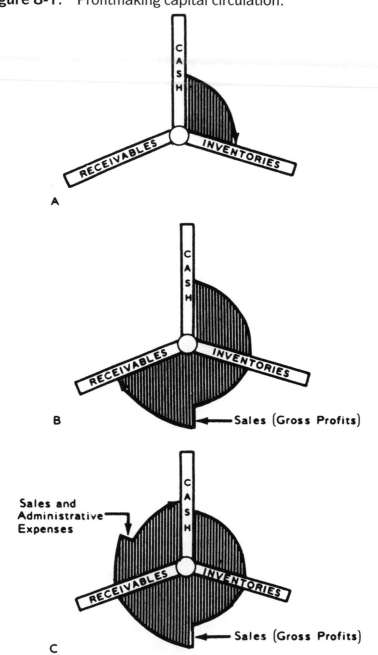

APPLYING THE TURNOVER PRINCIPLE

The circulation of capital funds in a customer's business takes on meaning only when it relates to time. Since capital funds turn over in a complete cycle from cash to inventories, then to receivables, and finally back into cash again, their rate of flow can be measured as the rate of turnover. The faster the turnover, the greater the profit.

Stepping up a customer's turnover rate through profit improvement is the consultative sales representative's most important function. Unless your profit projects are by and large directed to improving the turnover of the capital employed in your customer's business—especially the capital that is in the form of inventories—you cannot accomplish your mission.

As with all products, the principle of turnover is crucial to maximize the value of the PIP process. PIPs are capital. It must be turned as fast as possible in order to maximize profit growth. As inventory, PIPs represent a cost. Only by being closed can their cost be reclaimed and their value begin to be realized.

PIPs in inventory account for two kinds of cost. One is the sunk cost of their manufacture. The other is the opportunity cost of remaining unsold. But PIPs do not just sit in inventory. They are perishable, losing their net present value to obsolescence or competitive replication. Their half-life grows shorter daily.

Turnover generally offers more opportunities than any other strategy for profit improvement. The most common way to improve turnover rate is through increased sales volume and lowered operating fund requirements. In some situations, turnover may be improved by decreasing sales or even increasing the investment in operating assets.

You are in excellent position to help improve a customer's turn of circulating capital since, as Figure 8-2 shows, the drive wheel that rotates capital is sales. You must continually search for the optimal relationship between your customer's sales volume and the investment in operating funds required to achieve it. At the point where the optimal relationship exists, the turnover rate yields the best profit.

Figure 8-2. Profitmaking turnover.

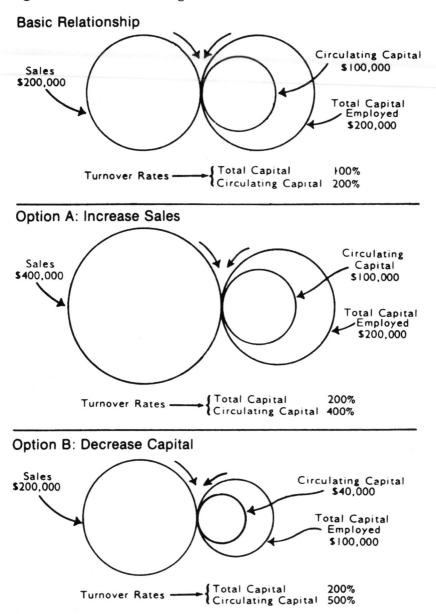

Basic Relationship

Sales
$200,000

Circulating Capital
$100,000

Total Capital
Employed
$200,000

Turnover Rates → { Total Capital 100%
Circulating Capital 200%

Option A: Increase Sales

Sales
$400,000

Circulating
Capital
$100,000

Total Capital
Employed
$200,000

Turnover Rates → { Total Capital 200%
Circulating Capital 400%

Option B: Decrease Capital

Sales
$200,000

Circulating Capital
$40,000

Total Capital
Employed
$100,000

Turnover Rates → { Total Capital 200%
Circulating Capital 500%

In Figure 8-2, the circumference of the sales wheel represents $200,000 worth of sales during a twelve-month operating period. The sales wheel drives a smaller wheel representing circulating capital. The circumference of the circulating wheel equals the amount of dollars invested in working funds, in this case $100,000. Enclosing the circulating capital wheel is a larger wheel, also driven by sales, that represents the total capital employed. It includes the circulating capital of $100,000 plus another $100,000 invested in plant and facilities. Thus the circumference of the wheel representing total capital employed is $200,000, equal to the sales drive wheel.

When annual sales are $200,000 and total capital employed in the operation is $200,000, the annual turnover rate of total funds invested is 100 percent, or one turn per year. The portion of the total that is circulating capital, amounting to $100,000, turns over at the rate of 200 percent, or twice a year.

Each of the three elements of circulating capital—cash, receivables, and inventories—has its own individual turnover rate. Inventory turnover is calculated according to the number of months' supply on hand. A six months' supply represents two turns per year, or a 200 percent annual turnover rate. Turnover of receivables is expressed as the number of days' business outstanding. If ninety days of business are outstanding, the receivables turnover is four turns per year, or 400 percent.

Since circulating capital increases every time it completes one turn, your job is to find ways to increase customer turnover through the use of your product and service systems. You can exercise two options for improving turnover. One way, option *A*, is by increasing sales. The other way is by decreasing the amount of money invested in circulating capital, option *B*. Figure 8-2 shows an opportunity to double customer sales to $400,000 per year without increasing the $200,000 of total funds employed in the business. This is option *A*. The turnover rate is increased from 100 to 200 percent. At the same time, the turnover rate of circulating capital increases from 200 to 400 percent.

If the consultant cannot increase the customer's sales, option *B* offers an alternative opportunity to improve turnover. Even though sales remain at the same annual rate of $200,000, turnover can be increased if total capital employed is reduced from $200,000 to $100,000. This includes a parallel reduction in circulating capital from $100,000 to $40,000. These reductions help the consultant improve the turnover rate of total capital employed from 100 to 200 percent and that of circulating capital from 200 to 500 percent. This strategy for improving turnover means that the operating funds of the customer's business are being worked harder.

The profit improvement created by options *A* and *B* can be readily appreciated by multiplying the increase in funds generated at each turn of the operating cycle by an increasing number of turns. If the operating profit from one turn in the basic relationship shown in Figure 8-2 is $50,000, the profit realized by option *A* is doubled to $100,000. In option *B*, profit remains at $50,000, but $100,000 of funds are released from operations that could be used to generate additional business or reduce indebtedness.

Opportunities abound for improving a customer's turnover. The reason is simple. The sum total of funds employed in a customer's business represents the many individual funds that make up circulating and fixed capital. An improvement in the turnover of any one of these funds correspondingly improves the turnover of the total funds employed. Therefore, you can zero in on any component of a customer's "turnover mix" without having to consider any of the others or their sum total. For example, improvement in the turnover of any single item in a customer's inventory—including your own product—improves total turnover and consequently contributes to profit improvement.

APPLYING THE CONTRIBUTION MARGIN PRINCIPLE

The key to profits is contribution margin—how much margin each product line or business unit contributes to a customer's total profits. Affecting a customer's contribution margins is a key objective of Consultative Selling. There are two ways to do this. You can help increase sales volume at the current contribution margin. Or you can help increase contribution margin at the current volume of sales.

Figure 8-3 shows how contribution margin works. It is calculated by subtracting variable costs from sales revenues. In the example, a customer's total contribution margin is 9.5 percent. That means that each single dollar of sales is currently contributing a margin of 9.5 cents to cover the customer's fixed operating overhead of $221,000. It takes a lot of $1 sales to contribute enough 9.5 cents' worth of margins to cover $221,000 of overhead. Even when sales do that, the customer merely breaks even. That is where you come in. If you can increase sales or decrease the variable costs that subtract from sales revenues, you can improve customer profits.

The consultant's choices are shown in Figure 8-3. If you want to work on product line A, you can improve profits best by improving sales. While it has only a 17.3 percent gross profit, it also has a 9.0 percent contribution. Any increase in sales volume produces new profits. On the other hand, if you work on product line

Figure 8-3. Analysis of profit contribution by product line ($000).

		Product Lines		
	Total	*A*	*B*	*C*
1. Sales	$2,600.0	$1,742.0	$650.0	$208.0
	100.0%	67.0%	25.0%	8.0%
2. Cost of sales	$2,106.0	$1,440.0	$520.0	$146.0
	81.0%	82.7%	80.0%	70.0%
3. Gross profit	$494.0	$302.0	$130.0	$29.8
(1–2)	19.0%	17.3%	20.0%	29.8%
4. Wages	$221.0	$134.0	$65.0	$22.0
	8.5%	7.7%	10.0%	10.6%
5. Other	$26.0	$10.0	$13.0	$3.0
	1.0%	0.6%	2.0%	1.4%
6. Total (4 + 5)	$247.0	$144.0	$78.0	$25.0
	9.5%	8.3%	12.0%	12.0%
7. Contribution margin (3–6)	$247.0	$158.0	$52.0	$37.0
	9.5%	9.0%	8.0%	17.8%

B, you have to reduce its variable costs. Its 20 percent gross profit exceeds that of *A*. But it is making only an 8.0 percent contribution after variable expenses. If you can reduce its expenses, you can improve its contribution even without increasing sales volume.

Applying ROI and Payback Principles

When you present a PIP to a Box Two manager, what questions can you anticipate?

• *What is the net present value of this deal?* To get the answer, the manager discounts your proposal's future cash flow projections at the rate of his company's cost of capital. The manager then calculates the cumulative value of these cash flows in terms of today's dollars in order to arrive at their present value. Finally, the manager subtracts the investment you are asking from the present value to learn the net value.

• *What is the return on investment from this proposal?* To get the answer, the manager multiples margin by expected turnover. If margins have been declining and you propose to improve them, you can leave the rate of turnover alone. If you cannot increase margins, the manager looks to see if you are proposing to increase turnover.

• *What is the payback period on the investment that is being proposed in the PIP?* Payback calculates the return *of* the investment, not the return *on* it. The manager wants payback as soon as possible in order to limit risk and usually calculates it by dividing the initial investment by the projected cash flows. Alternatively, each period's cash flows may be added together until the investment has been covered.

Customer managers use a business shorthand to appraise your PIPs quickly in order to qualify them for serious consideration. They use two criteria in rapid-fire order to make a quick study of the key things they have to know up front:

1. How much money can they most likely earn if they invest in your proposals?
2. How soon will they be able to realize it?

These two quick screens tell them if they are interested in going further with you, which means finding out how sure they can be about the "muchness" and "soonness" you are proposing.

Criteria of "How Much"

Customer managers use three criteria of muchness to determine how much they will get out of an investment in one of your PIPs:

1. *Net present value (NPV)* indicates the net value of all the future cash flows you will help them earn over the commercial life of your proposals, discounted back to their present value today so they have a common denominator of value. Bringing future values back to their present value, which discounts them, is made necessary by the time value of money. A dollar in the managers' hands today is always worth more than the value of the same dollar in their hands tomorrow. All managers have a minimum NPV standard for accepting proposals. You must PIP them above the standard to merit consideration.

Net present value is the prime index of value. Consultative Selling is NPV selling. The improved profits that a consultative seller sells are improved NPV. Nothing else tells the seller or a customer the true value of what is going to be returned on the customer's investment.

Net income by itself, representing cash flow, ignores the cost of the assets required to generate added revenues. Revenues by themselves ignore their costs. Return on investment by itself can inflate the perception of the return when the investment is comparatively small.

2. *Return on investment (ROI)* indicates the ratio of a customer's total profit improvement to the total investment required to generate it. In order to do a deal, ROI must equal or exceed a

customer's minimum hurdle rate for incremental investments—generally two-thirds or more of the customer's cost of capital.

ROI is a ratio of the dollar income generated by a PIP compared to the dollars invested. IRR (Internal Rate of Return) is the form of ROI that is most commonly used in PIPping. It shows the average annual percent return from each dollar invested over the commercial life of a PIP, adjusted for the impact of time.

3. *Aftertax cash flows* indicate a proposal's profit after subtracting for taxes and adding back depreciation and other noncash outlays. Cash flow is net income, commonly referred to as the *bottom line*. Cash flow is vital to every business. It can be even more important than profits because it pays for the continuity of ongoing operations. Depreciation is the reduction in asset value from use or obsolescence. It is based on periodically writing down a portion of an asset's original value so that it can contribute to the reduction of taxes, thereby influencing aftertax cash flow.

Criterion of "How Soon"

Customer managers use *payback* as their criterion of soonness to determine how soon they will be able to recover their investment in your proposals. The payback period is computed by dividing the total amount of an investment by the expected aftertax cash flows. Payback is an important determinant of the relative merits of competitive proposals. Once payback has occurred, the customer managers are "clean," removed from risk. From that point on, their interests focus on the net present value, accounting rate of return, and aftertax cash flows of your proposals.

Criteria of "How Sure"

The soonness of payback is a key indicator of how sure a customer manager can be of receiving the muchness and soonness of a PIP's proposal. The sooner the payback, the surer the deal. The major contributors to sureness beyond payback are your norms, which validate your track record, and your PIPs' Cost-Benefit Analyses, which prove your Prescriptions.

ROI is an analytic tool that has three qualities in its favor for your purposes: (1) it is a fair measurement of profit contribution; (2) it is helpful in directing attention to the most immediate profit opportunities, allowing them to be ranked on a priority basis; and (3) it is likely to be readily understood and accepted by financial managers as well as sales and marketing managers of your customer companies.

Figure 8-4 represents the two formulas for calculating ROI. The formulas relate the major operating and financial factors re-

Figure 8-4. Return-on-investment formulas.

A. Options for Improving ROI by Improving Turnover

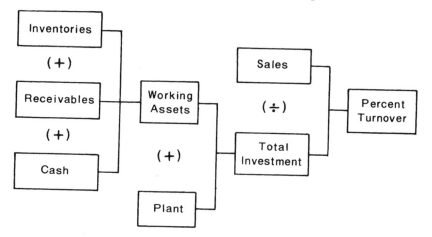

B. Options for Improving ROI by Improving Operating Profit

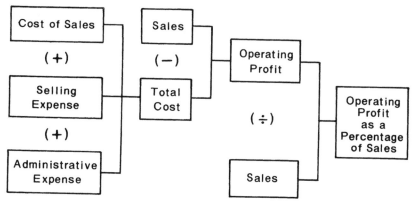

169

quired in profitmaking to the rate used to measure the profit that is made: the rate of profit per unit sales in dollars; the rate of turnover of operating funds, the funds required to finance business operations; and the total investment of capital employed, including working assets, plants, and facilities.

The customer's sole economic justification for investing in your profit-improvement projects is to earn a superior rate of return on the funds invested. This truism must be interpreted in two ways. One is in terms of income gained. The other is in terms of costs avoided in obtaining investment funds, costs of retaining such funds, and costs suffered by denying their use for alternative, potentially more profitable, projects.

Diagnosis is the heart of consulting. Diagnostic techniques based on ROI are the heart of diagnosis. As Figure 8-4 shows, ROI is the product of the rate of operating profit expressed as a percentage of sales and the rate of turnover. Any time you want to improve a customer's ROI, you must first diagnose a problem in the customer's operating profit rate or an opportunity to increase the customer's turnover.

Part *A* of Figure 8-4 shows the ingredients of ROI expressed as turnover. If you examine each of those ingredients, you will find profit opportunities that can improve turnover. You can, for example, recommend a project to reduce your customer's receivables. This reduces the amount of funds invested in working assets, thus reducing the customer's total investment base. As a result, you can improve your customer's profit without increasing sales volume.

Part *B* shows options for diagnosing profit improvement if your objective is to increase operating profit. You can recommend a project to lower the customer's cost of sales. This reduces total costs and enables the customer to show an increase in operating profit.

COMANAGING A CUSTOMER'S ASSETS

When customers invest their money to acquire your products or services, they obtain an asset. Their goal is to turn it over as quickly as possible so that it will revert to cash. Then they can reinvest in another asset with you and start the process over again. If they make good investments with you, they will end each investment cycle with more money than they started with. Asset turnover is the secret to making money. The more assets turned and the faster they turn over, the more money is made.

Accounts receivable and inventory are a customer's two major current assets. Current assets, by being turned over, are more quickly convertible to cash than are fixed assets. Anything you can do to speed up a customer's asset turnover in these two areas makes money for both of you. If you and a customer allow these assets to build up—if a customer's sales decline and inventories grow or if your customer's customers delay paying their bills— both of you are incurring the costs of lost opportunities.

Ideally, customers would like to have zero investments in accounts receivable and inventory. Every day that you can help them condense their collection period is money in the bank. Every additional turn of inventory also improves profits. An item that turns over 1.7 times a year sits in inventory approximately seven months before being sold. If you can help move it in six months, using the power of one, you can accelerate its contribution to earnings by one-seventh.

Asset turnover is especially important in selling to a customer's profit center managers. One of their key performance indicators is ROI, which is calculated by dividing their earnings by the investment in their asset base. The higher their ROI, the greater the investment that top management continues to make in their profit centers, and the higher the reward each center's manager receives.

The ROI of your customers is a good index of how good a comanaging partner you are. If you have the ability to affect inventory, but you let them stock out on their highest margin products, you are a poor comanager of your customers' assets. If you have the ability to affect collections, but you let their money languish in accounts receivable, you are more of a mismanager than a comanager. Increasing inventory turns and decreasing collection cycles make you better.

Whenever you make proposals to customers, you are challenging them to assess a risk. If you ask them to invest with you to expand their capacity to produce their existing products, you are offering them a median risk. All other types of investment have a higher or lower risk. Investments for replacement or repair are the safest. Past experience can accurately help foretell their probable cash flows. Cost reduction investments are somewhat riskier. No one can calculate the exact magnitude of their potential savings. The riskiest type of investment concerns new products or new market development, where neither the costs nor the revenues can be predicted with certainty.

As soon as customers invest with you, they incur an opportunity cost equal to the return they could have earned from an alternative investment of the same funds. The opportunity cost is in addition to the direct cost they pay you and the indirect costs they incur in implementation. The further away you take them from their median risk, where they know the return they can expect, the more risk-averse they will be and the more proof they will demand and the closer partnership with you they will expect.

Whenever risk increases, customers balance it against its return. In high-risk situations, they are more interested in whether the return is sufficient to justify the risk than the rate of return itself, however high it may be.

The risk-return trade-off is the basis of management. The only fully known sum of money in any transaction is its investment. Future benefits are always uncertain. As risk increases, the anticipated return must increase with it. If managers are confronted with two equal investments that promise a similar return, they will probably choose the investment with the lower risk—that is, the one with the higher net present value per dollar invested.

Where risk is equal or minimal, it is not a factor. Under these conditions, it is better to make an investment rather than let money sit idle—and thereby incur opportunity cost—as long as a positive net present value can be returned. This means that it must equal or exceed the customer's cost of capital. As long as it does either one or the other, the investment is acceptable. This is simply another way of calculating the worth of an investment based on its net present value. According to NPV, investing $50 million today for a stream of future cash flows with a value today of

$59.755 million is an acceptable investment. In effect, the customer is paying $50 million for an asset worth $59.755 million, gaining $9.755 million of new value. Since the NPV is well over zero, this is a good investment. If it were only zero, the customer's wealth would be unchanged and time would be wasted, consumed by opportunity cost.

Invoking Opportunity Cost to Accelerate Closing

Risk, no matter how minimal, increases over time. That is one reason why a dollar today is always worth more than a dollar in the future. Two other reasons why money has a time value are inflation and the opportunity cost that is incurred when money is not productively invested.

Because money has a time value, every dollar returned by an investment is worth less as time goes on. In the way that customer managers think about investments, they say that if I have 91 cents on hand today, I can invest it at 10 percent interest and it will grow into one dollar within one year. Is this the best deal available to me at this time? Can I get a better rate of interest anywhere else? Can I get a quicker payback? Can I get a larger return?

The fear of opportunity loss can be a powerful motivator to commit. Consultative sellers always calculate the value of a lost opportunity to invest with them, reminding their customers of how much it is costing them for each day, week, month, and quarter of deliberation and delay in comanaging a PIP. This puts a penalty on "missing out on a good thing" and, conversely, awards brownie points for biting the bullet.

In traditional vendor selling, time is always on the customers' side. The longer that a purchasing cycle is allowed to run on, the lower the eventual price. For this reason, delay is a more profitable strategy for customers than closing quickly. While prolonging price negotiation is in the customers' self-interests, the opposite is true for their suppliers.

Whenever vendors negotiate price, they lose twice. Loss of time is loss of money. As time is lost, vendors lose even more by discounting their price. Until they reach the price point where the customer calculates it will no longer be worthwhile to trade more time for an even greater discount, no close will take place.

Vendor prices are always initially unacceptable to customers because time will bring them down. Quick discounts rarely move customers to close. They know that the discounts will become successively deeper. Closure takes place when they perceive that each additional unit of waiting time earns them a diminishing return of discounted price.

When the value of time has such a different meaning for a customer and a supplier, there is no way that their relationship can be anything but adversarial. Talk of partnership by vendors is gibberish.

Consultative Selling makes partnership possible by endowing time with a mutual value. With a PIP proposal process, immediate closing benefits customers and suppliers alike. If customers stall closing a PIP, they incur a calculable opportunity cost from postponing today's profits until tomorrow. The dollars themselves can usually be made up; year five cash flow may have to wait to be recoverable until year six. But because money has a time value in addition to a dollar value, the worth of each dollar tomorrow will always be less than the worth of the same dollar today.

For the supplier, delay is also expensive. Any value proposed today begins to depreciate as soon as it is PIPped. PIPs are enabled by the application of technology, which is perishable. From commercialization forward, all technology is obsolescent. As its value depreciates, its once-exclusive ability to make a contribution to customer profits may become equalized or superseded by a competitive technology. As a result, a PIP's value proposition must be revised downward at the same time that its customer's opportunity cost is rising: It is lose-lose.

The unwillingness on both sides to absorb opportunity cost drives quick PIP closure. Each party is motivated by self-interest in wanting its money now. The customer wants to maximize the net present value of time. The supplier wants to maximize the net present value of technology. A waiting game is a losing game for both of them.

GUARANTEEING RESULTS AND GAINSHARING REWARDS

Once a PIP has been accepted, even before its value has been realized, the consultative sellers' customers are already counting on the new earnings they just contracted for. They will find sources of investment for the project's earned funds just as soon as the funds are available, not wanting to waste a minute in putting them to work. They will depend on their being available on time and in the amount promised. If they are not available, customers suffer a shortfall. They will also suffer a lost opportunity.

Since funds still "on the come" are already invested as if they were real as soon as they are proposed, failing to realize them can be a catastrophe. The funds are planned for. If they are not going to be delivered, the customer will be surprised. It is not necessary to say "unpleasantly surprised." Managers learn early in their careers there is no such thing as a pleasant surprise; all business surprises are unpleasant.

There is no substitute for guaranteed results. When you guarantee your solution, you are acting as a coguarantor, a cosigner of your proposal. Your Box Two partner is the actual guarantor. Your partner is the true receiver of corporate funds, choosing to invest them with you. This makes each Box Two manager the ultimate responsible party whose career success or failure is at stake and whose reputation as a "good manager" is enhanced or downgraded by your proposal's effectiveness. Simply by the act of endorsing your proposal and going public as its sponsor—your internal "economic seller"—customer managers are implicitly guaranteeing that they will return their company's funds plus a profit. When you partner with them, you inherit the same obligation.

Guaranteeing your results is the ultimate answer to the customer's question: How sure? By establishing a floor for your payoffs, it allows you to eliminate the ceiling on your reward. Once you achieve your guarantee, you can ask to share in any gains over and above it.

Gainsharing is an alternative to price. It is based on an understanding between a supplier and customer that their business together should be a mutual value exchange. The supplier should grow the customers by adding value in the form of increases in their revenue capabilities and cost savings. In turn, the customers should grow the supplier by adding value in the form of enhanced margins at high volumes.

A supplier and customer who cannot make money *with* each other—not *on* or *off* one another—cannot grow each other. If they cannot grow each other, they cannot partner, because mutual growth is what partners do day in and day out.

Gainsharing is the partnering strategy for growing value and for mutually participating in its gains. It rewards the partners' mutuality of objectives, their mutual strategies to realize them, and their mutual acceptance of risk. It positions suppliers as growth consultants whose essential capability is to add value. As an opportunity-seizing and problem-solving approach to doing business, gainsharing dedicates suppliers to wealth creation, not just to the creation of products or services. It puts them in the business of manufacturing and marketing wealth.

The emergence of a basis for gainsharing at Boeing illustrates the incremental but nonetheless progressive nature of the change. Originally, Boeing went into the market to "find the suppliers with the lowest bid and monitor them so they don't screw up." Then Boeing began to "find the suppliers who make the best product and make them part of the process." Boeing's emergence will be complete when it sets out to "find the suppliers who can create the most new wealth with us and partner with them by sharing the gains."

Gainsharing is neither a supplier strategy nor a customer strategy. Both benefit; neither incurs a downside. The mutual nature of the reward should drive both of them to gainshare whenever a unique value can be added to a customer operation that contributes to a superior gain.

Other factors along the lines of avoiding or diminishing negative outcomes also favor gainsharing and, in some cases, tend to make it inevitable:

- Few suppliers are able to recover enough margin on product sales to refertilize their R&D with sufficient funds to ensure continuous short-term innovation cycles. Product acquisition has become a cost-control function, pushing suppliers' price points inexorably downward toward zero cost.

- Few customers are able to achieve and maintain best practices as their industry's low-cost manufacturer or high-share market leader by relying only on standard solutions produced by their suppliers. Standard solutions yield standard practices. Yet no suppliers can afford to provide custom solutions at cost-controlled price points and still achieve low-cost supplier status for their own business. The only way to obtain funds for custom solutions is through gainsharing.*

- Person-to-person negotiation between customers and suppliers on price has become cost-ineffective, adding both direct and opportunity costs to the customer's cost-controlled process of acquisition and adding to a supplier's cost of sale. It is only a matter of time before it becomes unaffordable to both parties to allow sales representatives and purchasers to negotiate commodity transactions based on price. When human beings are involved in negotiations about exchanging value, gainsharing is the only affordable subject to debate.

Applying Your Intellectual Capital

Gains for sharing come about as the result of applications of one or more of three forms of capital:

1. Intellectual capital in the form of the expertise required to initiate and manage a profit-improvement project
2. Financial capital in the form of investment
3. Operating capital in the form of products, services, and systems

*The authoritative guide to sharing in the contributions made to customer profits is available in *Gainsharing™: Alternative to Pricing* by Mack Hanan and Jon Feinstein, (New York: The Greymatter Group Inc., 1999).

Applying intellectual capital to create profit-improvement projects, not simply stocking them with operating capital, is becoming increasingly recognized by suppliers as what their business is all about. But ideas in themselves are worth little, being nothing more than raw materials that rank at the bottom of the value curve. By adding values from application and implementation, information and education, and consultation and evaluation of results, intellectual capital can realize whatever opportunity it may have for capitalization.

The *gain* in *gain*sharing is net present value (NPV). It is calculated as the present value of a wealth creation project plus the worth of all future values when they are discounted back to the present. This takes into account the reduced value of money over time. In addition to NPV as the key indicator of gain, payback is a measure of the exposure to risk in realizing the NPV. The longer the payback, the greater the risk. A third indicator is the relationship of reward to risk that is calculated by the ROI.

Penetrating Your Customers' Value Chains

In order to share in the gains you contribute on a PIP-by-PIP basis, you must find a customer problem or opportunity that lets you realize three results:

1. The maximum gains from a product, service, or system application can be contributed.
2. They can be accumulated in the least time.
3. They can be accumulated at the highest level of cost-effectiveness.

As a consultative seller, you must seek out customers who can gain the most from your PIPs so that there is maximum gain for both of you to share. Customers who can gain the most are called "gain-sensitive." A customer can be gain-sensitive no matter where the business may be on an industry's value-creation curve:

- Customers who are ahead of the industry curve can be gain-sensitive because they want to stay ahead.

- Customers who are behind the curve must be gain-sensitive because they want to move up before they drop off.
- Customers who are in between are gain-sensitive because they must move up to become one of the top three competitors or face up to two business-altering options: consolidate by acquiring or being acquired, or vacate their market.

Fitting In as a Value-Adding Partner

If you want to gainshare instead of price—in Consultative Selling language, "propose an investment"—you must be able to answer the customer's question, "Where do you fit as a partner in the gains of my business?" In order to answer, you must know where you can add value. Since you are not offering yourself as a partner in the entirety of a customer manager's operation, your positioning is crucial in helping determine if there is a partnerable vacancy that you can fill.

- Suppliers who position themselves as *moneymakers* are fitting themselves primarily into a customer's sales, marketing, and distribution operations. They may also fit into the parts of a customer's product development, market research, manufacturing, or inventory control operations that affect sales. Moneymakers can range up and down value chains, intervening in operations where they are capability-specific for improving contributions of revenue.
- Suppliers who position themselves as *moneysavers* are fitting themselves differently into customer support and supply operations. Instead of acting as sales builders or market builders, they add value by reducing an operation's contribution of costs.

Of the two platforms for gainsharing—one to expand revenues and the other to reduce costs—the proposed gains from cost reduction are easier to calculate and propose than revenue improvements. Customers accept potential cost savings more readily than a prospect of newly generated revenues. Costs, being internal, can be better controlled. Markets, the sources of revenues, are more ephemeral since they are outside customer control and defy prediction. Besides, customers are almost always better at control than at expansion. Yet revenue improvements are almost always significantly greater contributions to gain for sharing.

SPECIFYING INSTEAD OF BEING SPECIFIED

As a consultant, you should be proposing improved profits as a result of solving customers' business problems by the application of your technology to their operations.

You are not selling your technology. Nor are you selling solutions to customers' business problems such as "improving materials flow" or "decreasing production backlogs." You are selling improved profits; they are your product, and your proposals must set them forth in their major specifications of how sure your customers can be that they will receive the "muchness" and "soonness" in your proposal. Customers will not have the comfort level to partner with you if only you are sure. Your sureness is unimportant. You must make your customers feel sure. Unless you do, they will tell you that they are not comfortable. If they stay that way, you will not partner them to sell for you.

There are many short-term comfortable partners. There are fewer long-term comfortable partners. But there are no long-term uncomfortable partners.

You make customer managers comfortable when you give them the evidence to prove where the return on their investment will come from and how it will flow. You may think, quite naturally, that the investment causes the return. Actually, it is the other way around. It is the promise of the return that causes the investment to be forthcoming, making the investment the result. If you do not make customers comfortable with the cause of their new profits first, they will be unable to envision a result.

When customers sign off on a transfer of funds to you, they are committing to incur an asset. They own something new. Its cost becomes a part of their balance sheets, increasing their indebtedness. The only valid trade-off for their debt is the added values they can receive from the improved operation, process, or function in their business that you will help them achieve.

To make this trade-off measurable, a consultative proposal is modeled after proposals commonly prepared by Box Two for presentation to Box One. When you present it to your Box Two partners, you will be playing their role. They will be playing the role of Box One. The more closely you replicate your Box Two partner, the more closely they will relate to you as partnerable and the more readily you will be accepted into their internal hierarchy.

You, like Box Two, will become a specifier of profit-improvement solutions. Box One, who allocates assets to maximize their profitable return, will sit in judgment of both of you. Together, you will follow the official business proposal approach: First, diagnose a problem or opportunity in business terms; second, prescribe a solution in business terms; third, prove how the solution works in business terms; and fourth, commit to controlling the solution to make sure it works in business terms—that is, make sure it improves the proposed amount of profits on time.

A consultant can find many relatively simple ways to specify profit improvement. If you sell to supermarkets, you can show each chain's central headquarters or even individual store managers how an improved planogram, substituting your brands for others or increasing the number and location of their shelf facings, may improve profit per case or per $100 of sales.

Profit improvement for a manufacturing customer may depend on improving the profits of dealers and third-party value-added resellers (VARs). By helping a customer's distributor organization increase its contribution—something the customer cannot directly control yet must nonetheless influence—you can help your customer raise the profit on sales made through channels.

A distributor's largest single investment is likely to be in inventory. The key to distributor inventory control is finding the minimum investment required to maintain adequate sales and service. One way of measuring the utilization of inventory investment is to compare distributors' inventory turnovers with their industry's average. Inventory turnover can be computed by using this formula:

$$\frac{\text{Cost of sales for one year}}{\text{Average inventory}} = \text{Inventory turnover}$$

If customers' distributors are in a business where the inventory turns an average of 4.5 times a year, or once every eighty to ninety days, you can help a distributor whose turnover is lower than average see their problem this way:

$$\frac{\text{Projected cost of sales}}{\substack{\text{Projected average} \\ \text{inventory level}}} = \frac{\$370,000}{\$100,000} = 3.7 \text{ Inventory turnover}$$

To help these distributors increase turnover to approach the 4.5 industry average, you will have to help them reduce inventory investment. To do this, you must first find out what level of inventory investment can yield a 4.5 turnover. Divide the distributors' projected cost of sales by the desired 4.5 turnover, which results in an $82,000 inventory. It now becomes clear that you can help the distributors achieve profit improvement by reducing inventory investment by $18,000. Then you can turn your attention to optimizing the inventory mix.

The consultant's best approach to inventory reduction is usually through product line smoothing. Distributors almost always carry too many items in their lines. An inventory burdened by too many items can cause a dissipation of the distributor's sales concentration, extra handling costs, waste through obsolescence or spoilage, and, of course, higher inventory carrying costs, higher insurance costs, and overextended investment.

To analyze a distributor's inventory, you can simply rank the products in the line according to their cost of sales and then compute their inventory turnover. Such an analysis could look like this:

- Products A, B, C, and D account for 57 percent of the cost of sales but only 34 percent of inventory. These products turn over inventory by an average of 6.2 times a year.
- Products E, F, G, H, J, and K account for 43 percent of the cost of sales but 66 percent of inventory. These products turn over inventory by an average of only 2.4 times a year.

The inventory turnover analysis in Figure 8-5 shows what it costs the distributor to carry inventory. By comparing the carrying costs of inventory to forecast sales volume, you can begin to learn more precisely what inventory the distributor should maintain. The first four products are apparently well controlled. They have an average turnover rate of 6.2 percent and 1 percent average carrying cost as a percentage of sales. You now know that you must concentrate on reducing inventory whose average turnover rate is only 2.4 percent and average carrying cost is 2.6 as a percentage of sales. This helps bring the distributor's inventory down to the $82,000 level that should contribute to the projected 4.5 inventory turnover.

Figure 8-5. Inventory turnover analysis.

Product	Percent-age of Sales	Average $	Percent-age of Average	Turnover	Carrying Cost as Percent-age of Sales
A	15%	$ 7,000	7%	8.2%	0.8%
B	17	9,000	9	7.0	0.9
C	14	11,000	11	4.7	1.3
D	11	7,000	7	5.8	1.1
Subtotal	57%	$ 34,000	34%	6.2	1.0
All other products	43	66,000	66	2.4	2.6
TOTAL	100%	$100,000	100%	3.7%	1.7%

MIGRATING INITIAL SALES

Key account penetration through Consultative Selling is a reciprocal process. Preliminary partnering makes possible initial entry at top-tier levels. Once entry has been accomplished, partnering should proceed apace so that migration opportunities open up beyond the initial sale. The purpose of preliminary partnering is to gain entry. The purpose of entry is to migrate, to penetrate a customer business in ever-expanding breadth and depth from your breakthrough point. The purpose of migration is to grow the customer's business and your business again and again.

In addition to the obvious benefit of providing ongoing high-margin sales opportunities, migration offers several other advantages. It helps amortize the investment in data collection. It helps develop new information sources about a customer business. It spreads awareness of your consultative positioning. And it helps deny opportunistic chances for competition to move in on a problem that you can, and should, solve. It helps prevent departnering.

Some migrations occur naturally—the solution of one problem leads progressively to the discovery of another, or a solution in one division stimulates customer interest about its transfer to a similar problem in another division. Other migrations take place only as a result of effort. You have to search out opportunities in the nooks and crannies of your customer businesses, relying on your customer process smarts to point up the most productive areas to explore.

The objective of penetrating a customer business in depth is to serve all major needs with your major products, services, or systems. This concept can be called maximizing "share of customer" as long as it is understood that it is not simply a volume criterion—it is a standard of the importance of your involvement. If you are significantly involved, you can become the preferred supplier of your customers' improved profits. Penetration in depth is inextricably tied to penetration in important areas of a business. Migration must be a selective policy whose aim is to consolidate your position as a profit improver of the most vital functions you can affect.

The ideal migration timetable makes improving profit in one operation the jumping-off place for improving profit in the next operation. In this way, you can extract maximum learning value from each experience. You can also avoid stretching your resources too thinly across more assignments than you can handle. It pays to remember that migration works both ways. One significant success encourages permission to try another. One significant failure discourages permission to try anything more at all.

Installing an initial system should therefore be regarded as planting the seed for follow-on sales opportunities, not the end of the sale. Once a sale has been made, the consultant has acquired a major asset: a more profitable customer. You can benefit the customer even further by additional profit improvement through one or more of three types of migration. You can offer to *supplement* the initial system with added value. Perhaps some value may have been sacrificed for financial reasons at the time the original system was approved. Or perhaps a greater need has become apparent only after installation. As a second type of follow-up, you can offer to *upgrade* the original system, up to and including the ultimate upgrading, which is total replacement of the system. Third, you can offer to *integrate* an entirely new complementary system with the initial system.

These profit-improvement opportunities are not mutually exclusive. You can use all three approaches in sequence with the same customer. First, you can supplement the entry system. Then, at a later date, you can upgrade some of the original system. Finally, a complementary new system can be integrated with the original one. Then you can recycle the sales approach by offering to supplement the new system, then upgrade it, and eventually integrate a third system with the first two.

This recycling strategy is illustrated by the following scenario. It begins *after* an initial system is in place and producing prescribed profit-improvement benefits.

Cycle 1

1. Supplement initial system.
2. Upgrade initial system.
3. Integrate a complementary new system with the initial system.

Cycle 2

1. Supplement new system.
2. Upgrade new system.
3. Integrate a second complementary system with one of the existing systems.

Cycle 3: Repeat Cycle 2 and turn it faster.

The incremental value of a consultant's relationship with a key account customer is simple to calculate. At any given time, it is the sum total of earnings from all of a consultant's Profit Improvement Proposals. A few proposals will probably be spectacularly successful. But for the most part, steady, modest success is all that is required.

Each proposal should be successful in its own right. Beyond that, it should also lead naturally into the next successful project. As your profit-improvement contributions accumulate in a value-adding chain, you are building equity. This equity consists of the value of the portfolio of PIPs you have installed in each account. The reward for good work is more work. By inviting you to remain in the game and try to improve profit one more time after each success, your customer is acknowledging a consultative partnership. As with all partnerships, "congratulations" is always followed by "you're vulnerable."

You, the consultant, are only as good as your last proposal. This should cause you to be financially conservative. Paradoxically, however, you will also have to be strategically daring in conceiving profit-improvement opportunities and planning to capture them. The net result of combining these two characteristics becomes the essence of your personal consultative style.

In planning to construct a profit-improvement portfolio, you should start small. At the outset, you must be content to make a single profit improvement in one business function or one product line in one account. Since the first proposal will probably be evaluated more critically than any of its successors, you must follow one injunction above all others: *The first time out, be successful.*

9

How to Sell
the Customer's Return

The penetration plan is your annual blueprint for getting into and staying in the business of a principal customer. The way you get in is by improving the customer's profit. The way you stay in is by continuing to improve the customer's profit, extending it to the solution of new problems, and never letting go.

The process for penetration planning requires answers to three critical questions that can determine up to 80 percent of your profitability on sales:

1. Who is my customer?
2. What can I do to improve my customer's profit?
3. What will my customer do for me in return?

The answer to the first question is crucial. Your customer is never a company as a whole, nor is it even a division. It is a specific business manager within a division whose costs you can reduce or whose contribution to sales you can increase. If you are IBM, your customer is not PepsiCo. Nor is it PepsiCo's Frito-Lay division. It is the manager of Frito-Lay's inventory control function, for example, whose contribution to Frito-Lay profits you can improve by improving that manager's performance in a key indicator, such as same-day shipments.

Planning to penetrate divisions or departments of customer companies is a far cry from vending commodity merchandise to purchasing managers on a price-performance basis. It is a totally different process: data-dependent rather than persuasion-dependent. Its database must therefore be structured to support the differences in sales strategy that a consultative approach demands.

Opportunity databasing hinges on one central concept: maximizing contribution. Two kinds of contributions are involved. One is your profit contribution to a customer. You must maximize it. The other is a customer's profit contribution to you. You must maximize that also.

The role of a profit maximizer differs from the role of a needs analyst or a benefit provider or a problem solver. All these are intermediate steps. Through needs analysis, the provision of benefits, and the solving of problems, profits become improved. This is the ultimate step. If it does not take place, all the intermediate objectives can still be accomplished, but they will be in vain.

High-penetration objectives—superior profit objectives for your customer and for you as well—are financial objectives. Nothing supersedes them. They must come first in your penetration plan because they are the purpose of the plan. The only reason to plan is to be able to set and achieve high financial objectives.

The objectives of your plan should be databased in the manner of the Fast-Penetration Planner:

1. The most likely profit contribution that will be made *by you* to each customer
2. The most likely profit contribution that will be made *to you* by each customer

"Most likely" profits are a conservative estimate. They are only somewhat more bullish than bearish. They represent the contributions that can be expected if your strategies work according to plan and if there are no important hitches that have not been planned for. In practice, they should come out just about right.

If you help customers improve their profits from incremental sales, you may have to adjust the gross profits by the customers' effective tax rate before you commit to an objective. If you improve customer profits by cost savings that can flow directly to the bottom line, you can calculate the profits as net incremental gain.

Only the net counts. Neither you nor your customers can take anything else to the bank.

The total annual contribution you expect to make to your customers is the sum of all the Profit Improvement Proposals you plan to install in their business functions during a year. The contribution your customers make to you is the sum of your profits from the sale of each proposal that is collectible during the same year. Two ratios are helpful to monitor how effectively your resources are being allocated to obtain each customer's contribution. One compares profits to the expenditures required to achieve them; this is return on investment (ROI). The second is the more traditional ratio of revenues to expenses.

DEVELOPING YOUR "WHAT-IFABILITY"

The ability to propose a steady stream of investment opportunities or, more correctly, return opportunities to your customer partners is the engine that drives Consultative Selling. Proposals mean business. They make money for you and your customers, keep your learning curve strong by giving you access to new sources of information about customer businesses, and keep your partnerships active, alert, and alive. You should always have a minimum of three proposals in progressive stages of development. The one that you are working on should be on the table, the next one should be heating up in the oven, and the third should be in the freezer awaiting defrosting.

The proposals that are in the oven and the freezer represent your inventory. Until you sell them, they run up opportunity costs for you and your customers. You should turn them over quickly.

A consultative seller is continually diagnosing problems and opportunities and what-ifing solutions. Asking the customers "what if?" invites them to play strategic Ping-Pong with you. Each what-if should provoke either a "how?" or an enhanced what-if from your partner, building on your proposal or coming at it from a different cut. By presenting your proposals as questions, you circumvent most of the defensiveness that causes adversarial rejections and refusals to buy in. Instead, you open your proposal to the customers, asking them in, so they can add their values to it and make it partly their own. Unless it becomes "theirs" in this way, they will not sell it with you. As long as your proposals remain "yours," you will be a vendor.

For example, consultative sellers might ask a supermarket chain: "*What if* you can acquire the equivalent of a $500,000 order each week without incurring a single dollar for cost of sales? You can, if you can eliminate out-of-stock opportunity cost in a single best-selling brand in your dry cereals sections."

Or they might ask the same supermarket customer:

What if you can offer your customers more advertised specials each week than your competitors can? In addition, *what if* you can also offer deeper price cuts on each of these specials? How much in new sales and profits can that earn for you each year, considering that every single dollar of new earnings will be net, because all costs of each special will be fully funded by us?

The funds required to support our contribution will come from savings of more than $90,000 per store annually.

On a per-store basis, the operating costs break down like this: For a store with gross weekly sales of $140,000, savings are projected as approximately $7,650 per month.

"What-iffing" is the driver of continuous improvement. No cost-benefit analysis, nor any PIP itself, is ever sacred. Consultative sellers are like Formula One racers. They are compulsive tinkerers, always testing. With the Formula Ones, the brakes are always being tested; so are the tires, the engine, and the steering. The correlates for consultative sellers are the investments and their returns, the net present values and the paybacks.

When your customers ask you how they can add the value you are proposing to their operation, they are opening your consultative sale. This answers the question "How do you open?" You do not. In Consultative Selling, the customer opens.

"How?" is the magic opener. It means, "How can I be empowered?" "How?" comes in several forms. Some are nonverbal: facial expressions such as raised eyebrows, furrowed forehead, pursed lips, or quizzical looks and sometimes nods. Fingers pulling at noses or earlobes, hands going to chins or backs of necks, and body leaning forward are additional nonverbal ways of asking "How?"

Verbally, a "how?" can be asked directly or indirectly as an expression of envy for your other customers whose profits you have improved, a revelation of wishes and wants that would constitute an ideal solution and how your proposed solution compares to it, or a request for added comfort expressed as a "Yes, but" reaction.

A qualified "how?" is often expressed in the form of pseudo-problems that are designed to test and probe your solution, your experience, or your commitment. Customers also may want to know what their competitors are doing—"I wonder how they do this?"—or why their own people have not applied a similar solution long ago.

A sales manager who is a devil's advocate is a valuable PIP partner in the early "what-if?" stage of formulating a proposal.

"You are going to propose that these customers make an investment with us of $1 million of new equipment—Why?" the manager can ask.

"What if it will enlarge their capacity enough to take on one new customer who can generate $1 million in incremental sales? This would give them a contribution margin of $25,000," you can answer. "You understand, I am using one customer just to demonstrate the power of one."

"First of all," the manager can ask, "Does this customer have a prospect who can do that? Second, what proof do you have that the return will fully pay back the incremental cost and yield the margin you propose?"

"If the customers' minimum acceptable return on an incremental investment of $1 million is 20 percent, closing a new customer for a 25 percent marginal return is a good deal. That's what we are really selling them: the income from one new customer they would not otherwise be able to serve."

PIPPING A PIP A MINUTE

Automating the proposal process makes it easy to produce a continuous series of PIPs, improving your productivity as a profit improver a hundredfold while reducing your PIP cycle times close to zero. The PIPWARE software program permits you to create "a PIP a minute." A new iteration of what-ifs can be prepared every sixty seconds in a professional business case format that can be closed right off the computer screen.

Figure 9-1 shows how PIPWARE software automates the calculations of costs and benefits whose work flow is shown in Figure 3-1. Figure 9-2 shows the ease of entering multiple *what-ifs?* into PIPWARE to calculate alternative outcomes.

The PIPWARE proposal is a ready-to-close request for an allocation of funds. It presents each proposal's business fit and its contribution to an objective that accelerates its realization in terms of net profits improved and annual cash flows. PIPWARE also documents each source of the customer's improved profits, the individual amounts contributed by revenue increases and cost savings, the rate of return on the customer's investment, and its payback period.

PIPWARE's cost-benefit analysis follows the same 1-2-3 rank order of internal customer requests for funds:

1. *The investment,* which is the "cost" in the cost-benefit analysis that includes the acquisition costs of the products, services, or systems you are proposing. If gainsharing is the method of customer investment, its amount can be bundled in the single line item on the Cost-Benefit Analysis called Total Expenses, or it can be highlighted as a Co-management Share deducted from net after-tax profits.

   How can you determine the optimal customer investment for the PIP's top line? The easy way is to apply your norms for past investments that have been made for similar solutions applied to similar customer operations that have yielded a satisfactory IRR (internal rate of return). Otherwise, a safe rule of thumb is that an optimal investment yields an internal rate of return that is no less than

Figure 9-1.   PIPWARE cost-benefit analysis.

Cost-Benefit Analysis

(RR)) Total Expenses (Net Cash Out)	Year 0	Year 1	Year 2	Year 3	Year 4	Year 5	Total
Total Expenses (Net Cash Out)	($6)	($296)	($473)	($364)	($299)	($299)	($1,737)
Total Benefits (Net Cash In)		$2,131	$2,131	$2,131	$2,131	$2,131	$10,655
Gross Profit Improvement:	($6)	$1,835	$1,658	$1,767	$1,832	$1,832	$8,918
Less Taxes	$2	($642)	($580)	($618)	($641)	($641)	($3,121)
Net Profit Improvement:	($4)	$1,193	$1,078	$1,148	$1,191	$1,191	$5,797
Cash Flow	($1,354)	$1,463	$1,450	$1,412	$1,389	$1,389	$5,748
Cumulative Cash Flow	($1,354)	$109	$1,559	$2,970	$4,359	$5,748	
Net Present Value	($1,354)	$1,330	$1,198	$1,061	$949	$862	$4,045

Internal Rate of Return: 103.8%

Payback (Months):   12

Tax Rate: 35.0%
Hurdle: 10.0%

Depreciation Method: MACRS
Amortization Method: Straight Line

Page: Cost-Benefit Analysis   ⬆ |◀ ◀ ▶ ▶| Edit   Preview   Present   Exit

193

Figure 9-2. PIPWARE what-if? options.

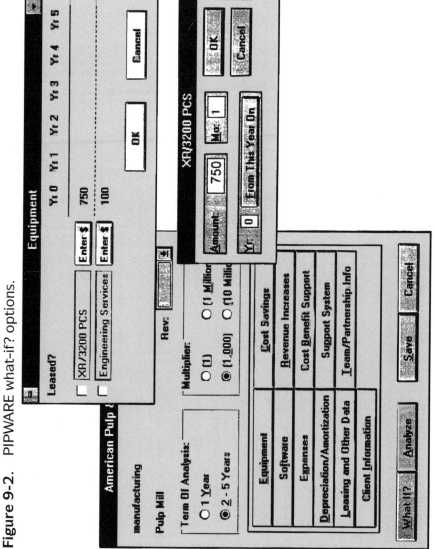

two times a customer's hurdle rate for incremental investments and not more than 100 percent.

Any lower IRR cannot be compelling. Anything higher means that you are leaving money on the table.

2. *The benefits,* which include all future cash flows from incremental sales revenues and savings that the investment can achieve from reduced variable costs such as labor, materials, maintenance, scrap, or downtime.

3. *The rate of return,* which compares the benefits to the investment.

A cost-benefit analysis is not a cost justification, which is what vendors use to sugarcoat their costs. In Consultative Selling, there are no costs to justify. Because consultative sellers realize a return that exceeds their costs, all costs become investments of current funds that are made to bring in future flows of cash that pay them back and keep accumulating to show a profit. A positive return means that cost is zero. Once you can show that an investment will cause a positive return, the anticipation of the return compels the customer to make the investment.

Through PIPWARE, you and your customer can preview in real time every likely consequence you can think of for each proposal option over the course of a profit project's commercial life in ways like these:

- *What if* we cycle the investment over two or more years instead of front-end loading it in year one—does that make our project more fundable?
- *What if* we cut back on the investment in year one to get to payback faster—does that make our proposal more closable?
- *What if* we cycle a series of short-term investments and plow back their returns so that we can self-fund 50 percent or more of each successive project—does that move us closer to the front of the line for approval?

Information technology applied to the PIP process has been revolutionizing Consultative Selling. PIPs are cycled faster. Mean-time between PIPs is reduced. Arithmetic errors are impossible to make. *What-if* iterations can be made one after another in order to get to the optimal solution. PIPs can be presented electronically or telephonically, sent by e-mail or posted on a Web site. They can be stored in a corporate retrieval system for sharing. Sales managers can access them for coaching and counseling on-line. Suppliers and their third-party business partners and strategic allies can co-PIP no matter where they are in the world. Multiple customer locations can be PIPped simultaneously.

Technology endows each consultative account manager with instant access to human and computerized data resources anywhere in the world. It permits daily, even hourly, virtual teaming that brings together the global expertise of technical, financial, and business development business partners as well as customers. It makes possible the remote ability to create an infinite number and variety of sales proposals on a 24/7 basis. It multiplies each consultative seller to act as a sales force of one.

The explosive power of information technology* is revolutionizing the strategy of business-to-business sales, the size, composition, and management of consultative sales forces, and the style and substance of the supplier-customer relationship. New definitions are being crafted for what constitutes best practices in terms of sales productivity percentages and revenue-to-investment ratios, for customer contribution and share of market penetration, for historic standards such as cost of sales, selling cycles and quotas, and for the social and political contexts of the consultative sales call.

All earlier forms of account management, symbolized by the vendor sales representative who is typically product centered, geographically bound, information constrained, and limited by the clock and custom to less than 20 percent of his or her total time actually spent in selling, are endangered species. They are today's

---

*The authoritative guides to the empowerment of Consultative Selling by information technology are available in two publications by Mack Hanan (New York: The Greymatter Group Inc., 2002): *Consultative TekSelling*™, which prescribes how the reach, impact, and frequency of proposal presentation can be amplified by collaborative teaming, electronic databasing, and customer-integrated proposing; and *Consultative e•Selling*™, which prescribes how to convert the Internet into a high-value high-margin sales channel.

equivalent of the twentieth century's salesperson with a briefcase and a smile.

IT has become the enabler of PIP immediacy, continuity, and universality. In these ways, it acts as the multiplier of consultative sales force productivity. The number of "feet on the street" is meaningless. PIPs proposed and closed are what count.

PIPWARE mimics the consultative seller's thought process from the first moment of targeting a lead to agreeing with the customer on the single best solution to the problem or opportunity it presents. PIPWARE's built-in thinking goes like this: "Which of my customer's strategic business objectives can I fit into? What operation in a line of business or business function that I can affect must I improve in order to make a contribution to the objective? What is the revenue or cost target that my customer manager's performance is being measured on? What is the minimal improvement that will give that manager a significant competitive advantage? What is the most cost-effective solution to deliver the improvement?"

By tying each PIP to an objective of your customers' strategy, you enter into their business. In effect, you say something like this:

> Your business strategy commits you to internally finance the development of several new product line extensions. Here is a cost-effective way to bring in $25 million of incremental cash flow over the next five years. This will pay for your total R&D costs plus a third of your test marketing for three line extensions.

Business fit should be as customer-specific as you can make it. If you were PIPping ALCOA, for example, when Paul O'Neill was chairman and you read in his annual report's president's letter that ALCOA was tightening capital spending and attempting to reduce costs across the board, you could present your PIP as fitting his objectives like this:

> "This proposal accelerates ALCOA's strategic business objective of increasing sales revenues and increasing

197

fixed asset turnover without adding to capital expenditures, and at the same time, decreasing unit costs."

PIPPING TO OUTSOURCERS AND OEMS

End-user customers become nonusers and noncustomers when they outsource an operation to a third-party provider. The outsourcer—or the insourcer, if a customer's operation is managed internally by the third party—becomes the customer for the products, services, or systems that the original customer no longer needs to purchase, install, maintain, or upgrade. When this happens, the outsourcer becomes the decision maker.

In order to ensure the cost-effectiveness of the operations they manage on their customers' behalf, oursourcers buy low. Since customers rarely know and hardly ever care about the names of suppliers an outsourcer does business with, outsourcers are the ultimate price shoppers. Any supplier who meets their specifications is immediately commoditized. In much the same way as an original equipment manufacturer obscures the component parts that are embedded in the final product, supplier brand names become subsumed in an outsourcer's sytem.

At one time, Electronic Data Systems (EDS), an outsourcer of information technology, said that the hardware components incorporated in its systems came from an Asian Pacific supplier named "Hu Kares."

Selling to outsourcers presents a situation where name, reputation beyond the consistent ability to meet specifications, or even competitive edge in technological bells and whistles counts for nothing that will compel a margin that is much above cost. The only differentiation that is meangiful is the power to make a unique contribution to the outsourcers' profits. This requires the ability to lower the outsourcers' operating cost of their system or find a way to help them earn more revenues from it.

If an operating cost can be reduced, the outsourcers can make more money on their contract with the customer whose facility they are managing. Without raising their fee, they can make a higher margin. The added value contributed by the incremental margin is PIPpable as the basis for a supplier's own improved margin.

If operating performance can be increased, the outsourcers can benefit from the constructive addition of new capacity to the system. This may make the system more productive for the customer without having to ask for an added investment to enhance it: more work may be able to be processed or more goods may be produced for sale. This may allow the outsourcers to raise their fee based on the added value or to provide a greater gain in which they can share.

Enlarging a system's capacity may also permit the outsourcers to sell the incremental time or output to other customers and share in the gain with their customers. This expanded revenue stream is PIPpable for its improved profits.

PIPping outsourcers follows the basic Consultative Selling strategies of reducing operating costs and increasing revenue inflows. Because product is irrelevant, no other strategy can command margin. In the outsourcers' frame of reference, where all products are equal and all sources of supply are opaque to their customers, margin must come from contribution to outsourcer profit rather than contribution to performance. Any unique performance benefit over and above specification has no intrinsic worth unless it can be PIPped as a profit improver.

Because outsourcing can be highly intensive in capital and labor, it is tempting to think of its practitioners as traditional managers of processes and facilities. But outsourcing is essentially a financial service business; its principal capital is financial capital. Outsourcers must therefore be sold to on the basis of bottom-line profits from savings on their committed investments or top-line income from new and unexpected revenues.

If you sell to Original Equipment Manufacturers (OEMs), you have a two-pronged sales mission. First, you must sell an OEM to incorporate your product as a component in its equipment. Then you must counsel the OEM how to maximize the value your product adds to its equipment by realizing improved profits from its sales.

For a process control manufacturer, a PIP's "what-ifs?" could include these benefit categories:

• Reduced time costs by shorter installation time, reduced production costs by requiring less labor for installation, and reduced downtime costs due to simplicity of construction.

• Increased revenue opportunity from high-margin sales by the ability to offer customers lower maintenance costs, improved yield, reduced scrap as a result of more precise control that increases the amount of marketable product, and enhanced quality.

In order to help OEMs maximize the benefits of your process controls when they sell their equipment to end-users, you can pre-PIP the OEMs' sales by what-ifs? in categories like these:

• Saves end-user energy costs by maintaining uniform temperatures, reduces environmental penalties, saves rework costs, and saves on space utilization.

• In the revenue area, gets more of an end-user's marketable product shipped and billed faster and provides premium-price opportunity based on standardized quality of an end-user's products.

RELATING HIGH MARGINS TO HIGH VALUES

The ability of Consultative Selling to command high-margin price points for products, services, and systems is documented by cost-benefit analysis. The objective of analysis is to derive a customer's economic benefits; the benefits can then drive the costs, which compose the investment required to generate them. In the cost-benefit process, the customer's investment is a function of the supplier's benefits. Benefits are the cause of the customer's paying out an expense, not the result.

Figures 9-3 and 9-4 show how iterative what-iffing can bring an investment into commensurate alignment with its return. This ensures the supplier's margin while the customer still gets a good deal.

The two figures represent consecutive iterations of what-if price strategizing. In each case, the supplier is the same provider of a collaborative software system that allows geographically separated product developers to use their corporate intranet to cooper-

Figure 9-3. What-iffing a $250,000 price point.

Cost Benefit Analysis

(000)	Year 0	Year 1	Month	Year 2	Month	Year 3	Month	Year 4	Month	Year 5	Month	Total	Leased
Investment (Capitalized/Amortized)													
Amortized Expenditures													
Software 1	($250)	($25)	0	($25)	0	($25)	0	($25)	0	($25)	0	($375)	N
Subtotal	($250)	($25)		($25)		($25)		($25)		($25)		($375)	
Total Cap./Amort	($250)	($25)		($25)		($25)		($25)		($25)		($375)	
Investment (Expenses)													
Expenses													
Consulting	($250)	($100)		($100)		($100)		($100)		($100)		($750)	N
Subtotal	($250)	($100)		($100)		($100)		($100)		($100)		($750)	
Leasing Costs		$0		$0		$0		$0		$0		$0	
Depreciation:		$0		$0		$0		$0		$0		$0	
Amortization:		($55)		($60)		($65)		($70)		($75)		($325)	
Total Expenses:	($250)	($155)		($160)		($165)		($170)		($175)		($1,075)	

(continues)

Figure 9-3. (Continued).

(000)	Year 0	Year 1	Month	Year 2	Month	Year 3	Month	Year 4	Month	Year 5	Month	Total	Leased
Benefits (Net Cash In)													
Revenue Increases													
Revenue Increases		$4,000		$11,200		$20,560		$26,644		$33,641		$96,045	
Subtotal		$4,000		$11,200		$20,560		$26,644		$33,641		$96,045	
Cost Savings													
Cost Savings 1		$480		$624		$811		$933		$1,073		$3,921	
Subtotal		$480		$624		$811		$933		$1,073		$3,921	
Total Benefits:		$4,480		$11,824		$21,371		$27,577		$34,714		$99,966	
Profit Improvement (PI)													
Gross PI:	($250)	$4,325		$11,664		$21,206		$27,407		$34,539		$98,891	
Less Taxes:	$100	($1,730)		($4,666)		($8,482)		($10,963)		($13,816)		($39,556)	
Net PI:	($150)	$2,595		$6,998		$12,724		$16,444		$20,723		$59,335	
Add Back Deprn:	($250)	$30		$35		$40		$45		$50		($50)	
Cash Flow	($400)	$2,625		$7,033		$12,764		$16,489		$20,773		$59,285	
Cum. Cash Flow	($400)	$2,225		$9,258		$22,022		$38,511		$59,285			
NPV	($400)	$2,386		$5,813		$9,589		$11,262		$12,899		$41,550	
IRR:	798.1%												
Payback (Months): 2													
Tax Rate	40.0 %												
Hurdle:	10.0 %												
Amortization Method.		Straight Line											

202

Figure 9-4. What-iffing a $1 million price point.

Cost Benefit Analysis

(000)	Year 0	Year 1	Month	Year 2	Month	Year 3	Month	Year 4	Month	Year 5	Month	Total	Leased
Investment (Capitalized/Amortized)													
Amortized Expenditures													
Software 1	($1,000)											($1,000)	N
Subtotal	($1,000)											($1,000)	
Total Cap./Amort	($1,000)	$0		$0		$0		$0		$0		($1,000)	N
Investment (Expenses)													
Expenses													
Consulting	($250)	($100)		($100)		($100)		($100)		($100)		($750)	N
Software Main		($100)		($100)		($100)		($100)		($100)		($500)	N
Subtotal	($250)	($200)		($200)		($200)		($200)		($200)		($1,250)	
Leasing Costs	$0	$0		$0		$0		$0		$0		$0	
Depreciation:	$0	$0		$0		$0		$0		$0		$0	
Amortization:	($200)	($200)		($200)		($200)		($200)		($200)		($1,000)	
Total Expenses:	($250)	($400)		($400)		($400)		($400)		($400)		($2,250)	

(continues)

Figure 9-4. (Continued).

(000)	Year 0	Year 1	Month	Year 2	Month	Year 3	Month	Year 4	Month	Year 5	Month	Total	Leased
Benefits (Net Cash In)													
Revenue Increases													
Revenue Increases		$2,000		$7,000		$13,940		$17,362		$21,430		$61,732	
Subtotal		$2,000		$7,000		$13,940		$17,362		$21,430		$61,732	
Cost Savings													
Cost Savings 1		$480		$624		$811		$933		$1,073		$3,921	
Subtotal		$480		$624		$811		$933		$1,073		$3,921	
Total Benefits:		$2,480		$7,624		$14,751		$18,295		$22,503		$65,653	
Profit Improvement (PI)													
Gross PI:	($250)	$2,080		$7,224		$14,351		$17,895		$22,103		$63,403	
Less Taxes	$100	($832)		($2,890)		($5,740)		($7,158)		($8,841)		($25,361)	
Net PI:	($150)	$1,248		$4,334		$8,611		$10,737		$13,262		$38,042	
Add Back Deprn:	($1,000)	$200		$200		$200		$200		$200		$0	
Cash Flow	($1,150)	$1,448		$4,534		$8,811		$10,937		$13,462		$38,042	
Cum. Cash Flow	($1,150)	$298		$4,832		$13,643		$24,580		$38,042			
NPV	($1,150)	$1,316		$3,747		$6,620		$7,470		$8,359		$26,362	
IRR:	240.5 %												
Payback (Months): 10													
Tax Rate	40.0 %												
Hurdle:	10.0 %												
Amortization Method.	Straight Line												

atively build "more better new products faster and cheaper." The eventual cost-benefit analysis will be the engine of a Profit Improvement Proposal to be presented to a manufacturer's new product development manager.

The benefits to be quantified are primarily the increased revenues from getting the manager's forthcoming new product to market faster than competition. In this way, greater volume at higher margins can be creamed from early adopters. As a result of collaboration, the product should also come closer to best-of-breed performance and thereby enable a greater contribution to customer profits. Cost savings are expected from a reduced innovation cycle, and lower selling costs should be achievable with a more advantageously designed and engineered product.

Both iterations of the analysis assume a 20 percent increase in year-one revenues over the customer's original projection of $20 million, followed by a 30 percent increase in years two and three. The rate of increase drops to 15 percent in years four and five as competitive replication and obsolescence start to erode net present value.

Margins are also projected to increase by 10 percent over plan in year one. Their rate of increase declines to 5 percent in years two and three and to 3 percent thereafter.

Figure 9-3 bases its analysis on a price point of $250,000 per system plus annual maintenance, upgrading, and consultation. This yields total benefits over five years of almost $100 million. The customer's IRR is 798 percent.

In the belief that an IRR of 798 percent is a philanthropic donation and not a business deliverable, a second iteration shown in Figure 9-4 costs out the system at a price point of $1 million: four times the amount of the customer investment in Figure 9-3. Total benefits over five years are reduced to $66 million at an internal rate of return of 240 percent.

While total expenses have doubled and payback takes eight months longer, Figure 9-4 shows that the supplier's PIP can be a good deal even at $1 million. This gives the supplier three options to locate a floating price point:

1. The supplier can accept the comparatively low margin that is realizable from an investment of $250,000. The resulting 798

percent IRR proves that it is unnecessary in order to compel the sale by being 788 percent in excess of the customer's hurdle rate.

2. The supplier can ask for the $1 million price and still exceed the customer's hurdle rate by 230 percent.

3. The supplier can ask a price anywhere in between $250,000 and $1 million and attach an incremental gainsharing schedule to it as an added margin equivalent.

The floating point that Consultative Selling makes of price gives the supplier, and all suppliers, considerable flexibility in making margin. Fairness is maintained as long as an IRR in the low three figures proves that the customer is receiving an otherwise unobtainable return on each dollar invested.

PLANNING FAST PENETRATION

Objectives are a plan's purpose. Strategies are the methods of achieving objectives. In Consultative Selling, strategies are packaged in PIPs. Each proposal represents a strategy to improve customer profit by solving a cost or sales problem. If the customer is a not-for-profit organization or a government agency, proposal strategies focus on reducing costs and improving the dollar value of productivity. Either way, the mix of strategies must make a measurable impact on customer profit or operational performance, or both.

PIPs are the sales vehicles for penetration strategies. They are designed to penetrate the customer's business at high-level points of entry. Each proposal contains a strategy for solving a specific customer problem or realizing a specific opportunity. The sum total of profits contributed by each year's proposals constitutes the value added by Consultative Selling.

Many vendors remain in denial. At Motorola, Jim Caile of the Cellular Subscriber Group is still trying "to figure out how to put value back in the hardware." Motorola's Two-Way Radio people are doing the same, even though value has long ago been commoditized out of the hardware and relocated into customer operations. For a plant of Cummins, Motorola discounted a sale of its factory floor radios down to $100,000. Within the first twelve months, Cummins had saved $1.20 million in downtime costs by speeding up maintenance and reallocating raw materials and labor. In return for selling the performance value of its radios instead of the financial value of their application, Motorola came away with only a fraction of the 12 to 1 value-to-investment ratio of the radio system's contribution to improved profits.

Consultative Selling makes vendor selling schemes obsolete. Even when vendors "earn the right" to sell upstairs, they have nothing to sell to a customer manager who opens by asking, "What have you got for me?" The vendor's typical response is a valueless value proposition that cannot price the investment because it cannot value the return.

NCR offers a valueless value proposition when it says, "NCR is your knowledgeable, safe, and innovative partner with proven experience." What is the value to a customer of NCR's "unmatched knowledge and expertise"? What is the added value of making "the safe choice"? NCR does not say.

Digital Equipment was typical of valueless proposers when it put forward characteristics of itself that may enable value but contribute no quantifiable value in themselves:

- "Proven track record"
- "Reliability and confidence"
- "Considerable expertise"
- "Diverse set of capabilities"
- "Customized approaches to addressing needs"
- "Commitment to implementation"

A single number—the most likely improvement in a customer operation's contribution to profits—is worth all these words. In addition, it is a true value proposition.

There are three steps to take before you can propose profit improvement:

1. Analyze a customer's business position.
2. Position penetration strategies.
3. Pinpoint penetration opportunities.

Analyzing a Customer's Business Position

A customer's business position determines your sales strategy. Each position presents a different penetration challenge.

1. *Penetrating a growing customer.* A growing customer is sales-driven. If you want to affect the sales function, you must increase its productivity so that it can generate more profits per sale or yield added profits from incremental sales. If you cannot affect sales but you can only reduce costs, the savings you achieve for a customer must be valued for their ability to support more sales. Your entire penetration strategy must focus on improving the customer's profit by increasing sales.

2. *Penetrating a mature customer.* A mature customer is driven from two directions at once. Sales must be increased, but not if this requires increased costs. If projected sales fail to result, the customer's stability can be threatened. Costs must be reduced, but not if this reduces sales or market share. If sales fall, the customer's stability can be threatened. Your penetration strategy can focus on improving profit through sales increases or cost decreases, but it must avoid the unaffordable risk of increasing costs or decreasing sales in the process.

Positioning Penetration Strategies

The purpose of analyzing a customer's business position is to be able to custom-tailor your sales penetration. If a customer is growing or stable, you must present yourself as an improver of profit on sales. If the customer is declining, you must present yourself as a reducer of costs.

Unless your sales position coincides with the customer's business position, you can never create a partnership in profit improvement. The customer will not understand where you are coming from in your proposals. You, in turn, lacking a sense of your customer's objectives, will not know where the customer is going. As two unknowns, you will be talking past each other; you will be proposing to yourself.

To ensure that your sales positioning is in gear with how your customer is positioned, your penetration strategy should be preceded by a positioning statement. Here is a model statement:

> In our penetration of the manufacturing functions of the ABC Company's XYZ Division, a stable business, we position ourselves as the manufacturing vice president's partner in profit improvement primarily by means of the reductions in cost we can deliver through our quality control system. We also show how enhanced product quality can help improve profit through incremental sales.

Pinpointing Penetration Opportunities

A customer's inability to bring down a cost or need to increase profitable sales volume are business problems. Accordingly, they can be your sales penetration opportunities. In order to find out, you will have to identify them and then put dollar values on them and on the most cost-effective solutions.

Opportunities to penetrate a key account have a special genesis. A penetration opportunity does not automatically come into being simply because a customer has a problem and you happen to have a solution for it. Discovery is not opportunity. To determine whether a penetration opportunity exists, you must first analyze three specific dollar values.

1. *The dollar value of the customer's problem.* How significant is it? Is it making a significant negative contribution to customer profit? Does it justify a significant expenditure for solution?
2. *The dollar values of the profits from your solution* that will accrue both to you and to your customer. How significant are they? When will they begin to flow? How long before their total amount finally accrues?
3. *The dollar values of the costs of your solution* that will be incurred both by you and by your customer. How significant are they? Are they all up front, or can they be paid for progressively out of the solution's improved profits?

Penetration opportunities are entry points. You should regard them as windows. An opportunity window opens for you when the following conditions are met:

1. The dollar value of the profits from your solution exceed the dollar value of the customer's problem.
2. The dollar value of the profits from your solution exceed the dollar value of the costs of your solution.
3. The dollar value of the profits from your solution exceed the dollar value of the profits from competitive solutions.

The first condition ensures that a customer problem is worth solving; that is, it is beneficial to solve. The second ensures that a problem is profitable to solve. The third ensures that your solution will be the preferred solution. All three conditions place the burden of proof squarely where it belongs—on your ability to create the most profitable solutions to customer problems in the business functions you can affect. This is the supreme standard of performance for Consultative Selling.

Prescribing Solution Systems

A consultant's solutions improve customer profit in proportion to the consultant's skill in prescribing added value.

The ability to prescribe the right solution system the first time is a result of three factors. One is the consultant's experience. The second is expertise. The third factor is skill in solving customer business problems and helping capitalize on opportunities: in other words, helping a customer improve profit.

A system's combined advantage is expressed as a single benefit: profit improvement of the customer's business operations in which the solution is installed. This benefit is a partial function of system price. It is also a function of the system's return on investment. The ability of a system to yield a return on investment that exceeds price endows it with premium-price capability.

Prescribing a system and pricing it for high customer return are the two most demanding tasks of Consultative Selling. Together they determine the customer's value and the profit from the solution. Because they have such a direct effect on both value and profit, the acts of prescription and pricing are keystones of the consultant's selling proficiency.

The standard of performance for prescribing and pricing a solution is met when its system's premium price is accepted as a cost-effective investment in added value to meet customer objectives.

When consultants prescribe a profit-improvement package, they must follow the rule of "necessity and sufficiency." Components should be sufficient, but only those that are necessary to solve the customer's problem should be prescribed. This guideline helps protect consultants against underengineering or overengineering a system. If a system is overengineered, it may have to be overpriced; if it is underengineered, it may contribute to customer dissatisfaction and invite competitive inroads.

To avoid underengineering, you may have to incorporate equipment or service components from other manufacturers to round out some systems. At times, it is possible to market these components under your company's own brand name. This is the preferred way. But even if they cannot be branded, they should nonetheless be integrated into your systems if they are necessary to realize value objectives.

To be of maximum benefit to your customer and deliver maximum profit to you, a system should have turnover built into it— that is, one or more of its components should be consumable. This allows you to generate an ongoing razor-and-blades type of market for product-related services and consumable supplies by providing continuing sources of income for your business and continuing participation in your customers' businesses.

A basic rule of system prescription can be stated in this way: *To maximize profit, standardize the hardware and customize the services, software, and consumables.* When the nonhardware components are customized, a system's premium contribution can be accelerated. When frequent turnover of consumables is multiplied by premium price, maximum profits can result.

Deciding Which System to Propose

The return-on-investment approach is the most helpful tool for determining which of two or more systems to propose to a customer as well as how to price them. Two competitive systems illustrate how a choice is made.

1. *System A* is forecast to improve customer sales by $200,000 and yield a profit on sales of 10 percent, or $20,000. The investment required from the customer is $100,000.
2. *System B* is forecast to improve customer sales by $300,000 and yield a profit on sales of 10 percent, or $30,000. The same $100,000 of customer investment is required.

These two systems appear equally worthwhile in terms of their 10 percent profit yield on sales. But in terms of the return each system can achieve on the amount of customer capital it employs, System B is superior. With System B, $100,000 of capital can produce a $30,000 profit—a 30 percent return. System A also requires $100,000 of capital but can produce only $20,000 in profit, for a 20 percent return.

The difference between the two is the relationship of the improved sales volume to the capital employed. System A allows its capital to appreciate at the rate of 200 percent. With System B, however, the appreciation is 300 percent: It turns inventories into cash faster.

There is a shorthand formula you can use to determine ROI:

$$\frac{\text{profit}}{\text{sales}} \times \frac{\text{sales}}{\text{capital employed}} = \% \text{ return on investment (ROI)}$$

In the case of System A:

$$\frac{20{,}000}{200{,}000} \times \frac{200{,}000}{100{,}000} = 20\% \text{ ROI}$$

212

In the case of System B:

$$\frac{30,000}{300,000} \times \frac{300,000}{100,000} = 30\% \text{ ROI}$$

In this simplified approach, the first fraction calculates the percentage of profit on sales; the second fraction calculates the turnover rate. When the two are multiplied, the result is return on investment. Any improvement in the circulation of funds invested in a system's total assets, working assets, or any component part of an individual asset has a multiplying effect on profits.

A system's marketability lies in its competitive advantage: the value added by improving customer profit. This customer advantage becomes the system advantage in the minds of customers, who evaluate systems both individually and competitively. A system does more than offer a customer advantage; the system comes to "own" the advantage as its single most crucial selling point. This is *preemption,* a system's ability to seize an advantage uniquely to itself.

The competitive advantage of a system acts as its market selecting mechanism. It selects customers in two ways. First, it seeks out and qualifies the segment of a market that has the greatest need for the system's advantage. Second, it comes to represent the system by acting as a shorthand way of describing its incremental contribution. The customer advantage determines the market and documents the system's capabilities.

A system's customer advantage must conform to three requirements:

1. It must confer a superior added value over competitive systems, as well as over the option of doing nothing, in at least one important respect.
2. It must be at least equal to competitive systems in all other respects.
3. It must not be inferior to competitive systems in any important respect.

A competitive advantage can be an attribute of the system, or it can come from the way it is implemented, maintained, migrated, or marketed. The question of how much quality to build into a system therefore merits a minimal answer. Enough quality to deliver the customer advantage is enough quality. A maximum quality system as determined by the aggregate quality of its components may not be perceived as offering the maximum customer advantage. Minimal systems from the consultant's perspective are often preemptive systems from the customer's perspective.

The concept of competitive advantage is not just an argument against overengineering, overpackaging, or overcosting, although it speaks powerfully against all three. It is essentially an argument in favor of prescribing systems from a customer orientation. And it provides the direction for establishing a system's branding: the capture of customer preference because the *customer's profit is being improved best,* not because the *consultant's system is constructed best.*

Customers who use EVA, the Economic Value Added to their operations, as a criterion for what to acquire or apply to their operations are ready-made partners for consultative sellers whose value propositions are additive to the customer's EVA.

EVA is the sum of two components, the second of which is subtracted from the first to get the added value:

1. NOPAT (net operating profits after taxes), which is calculated by adding the cost of products manufactured to GS& A expenses (general, sales, and administrative) and subtracting the result from sales revenues. In order to improve the contribution of NOPAT to EVA, a consultative seller's PIPs must improve sales revenues or reduce either GS&A or the manufactured costs of products.
2. Cost of Capital, which is the sum of outstanding receivables plus inventories. In order to reduce the contribution of a customer's capital costs to EVA, a consultative seller's PIPs must reduce receivables or inventory.

In addition to increasing the contribution of sales revenues to NOPAT and decreasing the contributions of receivables and inventory to the customer's cost of capital, PIPs can also improve EVA by speeding up new product development, improving production scheduling, reducing scrap and rework, and cutting down on warranty expenses. These are all exemplary objectives of Consultative Selling.

Appendix A

HOW CUSTOMER MANAGERS BUDGET CAPITAL EXPENDITURES

When a capital expenditure is proposed, the project must be evaluated and the economic consequences of the commitment of funds determined before referring it to a budget committee for review or to management for approval. How are the economic consequences described best? This is done in two steps:

First, set up the project in a standard economic model that can be used for all projects, no matter how dissimilar to each other they may be.

Benefits − costs = cash flow

To describe the formula in accounting terminology:

Benefits:	*Projected cash revenue from sales and other sources*
Costs:	*Nonrecurring cash outlays for assets, plus recurring operating expenses*
Cash flow:	*Net income after taxes plus noncash charges for such items as depreciation*

Thus, if the model were stated in a conventional accounting form, it would appear as:

Add:	*Cash revenues projected (benefits)*
Less:	*Cash investment outlay and cash expenses (costs)*
Total:	*Cash flow*

The "benefits less costs" model is usually developed within the framework of the company's accounts and supported with prescribed supplementary schedules that show the basis of the projection.

COMPARING COSTS AND BENEFITS

It should be apparent that in setting up an economic model, the conventional accrual accounting concept, net income after taxes, has been abandoned. The established criterion is cash flow—net income after tax plus noncash charges.

The second step is to adjust the cash flow into relevant financial terms. The cash flow projected for each year over the life of the proposal has to be translated into financial terms that are valid; that is, the annual dollar cash flows must be translated into a common dollar value in a base year. This concept must not be confused with attempts to adjust for changes in the purchasing power of the dollar.

The calculations assume no significant erosion in the purchasing power of the dollar. Should this occur, the time-adjusted common dollar concept may require adjustments for the diminished real value (purchasing power) of future dollar payments. The common dollar value concept used in capital budgeting adjusts for time value only. This is achieved through the development of the concept of discounting and present value that will be examined in the next section. An examination of how a simple two-step model is developed will illustrate the rationale of this approach.

In the first step, we set up the economic model: Benefits minus costs equals cash flow. To complete this model, we need to identify in detail all economic benefits and costs associated with the project. Benefits typically take the form of sales revenues and other income. Costs normally include nonrecurring outlays for fixed assets, investments in working capital, and recurring outlays for payrolls, materials, and expenses.

For each element of benefits and costs that the project involves, we forecast the amount of change for each year. How far ahead do we forecast? For as long as the expenditure decision will continue to have effects: that is, for as long as they generate costs and significant benefits. Forecasts are made for each year of the project's life; we call the year of decision "year 0," the next year "year 1," and so on. When the decision's effects extend so far into the future that estimates are very conjectural, the model stops forecasting at a planning horizon (ten to fifteen years), far enough in the future to establish clearly whether the basis for the decision is a correct one.

We apply a single economic concept in forecasting costs: opportunity cost. The opportunity cost of a resource (asset) is what the company loses from not using it in an alternative way or exchanging it for another asset. For example, if cash has earning power of 15 percent after taxes, we speak of the cash as having an opportunity cost of 15 percent. Whenever an asset is acquired for a cash payment, the opportunity cost is, of course, the cash given up to acquire it. It is harder to establish the opportunity cost of committing assets already owned or controlled. If owned land committed to a project would otherwise be sold, the opportunity cost is the aftertax proceeds from the sale. The opportunity cost of using productive equipment, transportation vehicles, or plant facilities is the incremental profit lost because these resources are unavailable for other purposes. If the alternative to using owned facilities is idleness, the opportunity cost is zero. Although opportunity costs are difficult to identify and measure, they must be considered if we are to describe the economic consequences of a decision as accurately as possible. An understanding of this concept of opportunity cost is probably the most critical to this economic analysis and is generally quite foreign to the manager.

At the end of the first step, we have an economic model for the project's life showing forecast cash flows for each year. In the second step, we convert the results into financial terms that are meaningful for decision making. We must take into account the one measurable financial effect of an investment decision left out in step 1: time. Dollars shown in different years of the model cannot be compared since time makes them of dissimilar value. We clearly recognize that if we have an opportunity to invest funds and earn 15 percent a year and we have a choice of receiving $1,000 today or a year from now, we will take the $1,000 today, so that it can be invested and earn $150. On this basis, $1,000 available a year from now is worth less than $1,000 today. It is this adjustment for time that is required to make cash flows in different years comparable; that is, discounting.

This time value of funds available for investment is known as the opportunity cost of capital. This should not be confused with the cost of raising capital—debt or equity—or with the company's average earnings rate. Like the opportunity cost of any resource, the opportunity cost of capital is what it will cost the company to use capital for an investment project in terms of what this capital could earn elsewhere.

The opportunity cost of capital is alternatively referred to as the minimum acceptable rate of interest, the marginal rate of interest, the minimum rate of return, the marginal rate of return, and the cost of capital. Whatever the term used, and they are used loosely and interchangeably, it reflects the rate the corporation decides it can be reasonably sure of getting by using the money in another way. It is developed through the joint efforts of management, which identifies relevant opportunities, and the controller, who translates management's judgment into a marginal rate.

Another simple economic concept must be introduced: incremental cost, sometimes called differential cost or marginal cost. By definition, it is the change in cost (or revenue) that results from a decision to expand or contract an operation. It is the difference in total cost. In performing the capital budgeting analysis, we deal with incremental costs (revenues) only. Sunk or existing costs are not relevant to the evaluation and decision.

DETERMINING PRESENT VALUE

Discounting is a technique used to find the value today or "present value" of money paid or received in the future. This value is found using the following formula:

Future dollar amount × discount factor = present value

The discount factor depends on the opportunity cost of capital expressed as an interest rate and a time period. Figure A-1 illustrates how discount factors are usually displayed. The discount factors are grouped according to the annual interest rate, expressed as the present value of $1.00, and then listed according to the year the amount comes due. The table should be read this way: When a dollar earns 10 percent per year uniformly over time, a dollar received at the end of the second year is equivalent to (worth) about 86 cents today.

To adjust the model's results for the time element, we discount both the positive and negative cash flow forecasts for each period at the company's marginal rate of return to determine their present value. This discounting process makes the forecasts equivalent in time. We can now add the present values of these cash flow forecasts to derive the net present value (NPV). The NPV is a meaningful measure of the economic consequences of an investment decision since it measures all benefits and all costs, including the opportunity cost of capital.

When the NPV of a proposed investment is determined, we are ready to decide whether it should be accepted. This is done by comparing it to the economic consequences of doing nothing or of accepting an alternative. The general rule followed in comparing alternative projects is to choose the course of action that results in the highest NPV.

Figure A-2 illustrates the cash flow forecasts and time-value calculations for a typical proposal to invest in a new project when the alternative is to do nothing, that is, to maintain liquidity rather than invest. A discount rate of 10 percent is assumed as the company's marginal rate.

Figure A-1. Present value of $1 at 10 percent.

Year	Present Value (Today's Value)
0–1	$0.9516
1–2	0.8611
2–3	0.7791
3–4	0.7050
4–5	0.6379

Figure A-2. Arithmetic of determining net present value (NPV).

Year	Benefits	Costs	Cash Flow	PV of $1 @ 10%	Discounted Cash Flow
0	$ 0	$ (500)	$(500)	1.000	$(500)
0–1	425	(200)	225	.952	214
1–2	425	(200)	225	.861	194
2–3	350	(200)	150	.779	117
3–4	250	(200)	50	.705	35
TOTAL	$1,450	$(1,300)	$ 150		$ 60 NPV

The proposed project will cost $500 in year 0, and cash operating expenses thereafter will be $200 per year for four years. Assume the cash benefits will be positive but decline over the four years and total $1,450. The cash flow is negative in the year of investment but positive in the succeeding years, and there is a net positive cash flow over the life of the project of $150 before discounting. When the cash flow forecasts are made equivalent in time by multiplying each annual cash flow by the present value of the dollar for each period, the time-adjusted cash flow is determined, and the NPV is found to be $60. The proposed investment is better than doing nothing because all costs are covered, the 10 percent opportunity cost of the corporation's funds is realized, and in addition, the project will yield an additional $60 return.

Figure A-2 indicates an NPV of $60. Depending on the cash flow and/or the discount rate, the NPV could be negative or zero. If the NPV were zero, the company would have projected earnings exactly equal to its marginal rate of 10 percent. If there were no alternative projects, and the only alternative were to do nothing, the project with the NPV of zero would be accepted because the company would earn its marginal rate of return. (As explained later, the NPV of zero would yield the discounted cash flow rate of return, that is, 10 percent.) If the NPV were negative because of an inadequate cash flow, assuming the same 10 percent marginal rate required by management, it would mean the project would earn less than 10 percent, and it would be rejected.

A number of evaluation methods are employed in capital budgeting; however, after critical examination of all methods, only the arithmetic developed in this simple model will be used to examine three methods used in evaluating capital budget proposals: (1) cash payback, (2) net present value, and (3) discounted cash flow rate of return (DCF-ROR)—sometimes referred to as the "internal rate of return."

Cash payback is commonly used by business managers evaluating investment opportunities, but it does not measure rate of return. It measures only the length of time it takes to recover the cash outlay for the investment. It indicates cash at risk. In our model there are costs of $500 committed in year 0. To determine payback, we merely add the unadjusted cash flow for each year and determine how many years it takes to get the outlay back. In the first two years $450 is recovered, and by the end of the third year $600 is recovered. By interpolation we find cash recovery to be approximately 2.3 years. It is obvious that the rational manager does not commit a large sum of money just to recover it. He expects a rate of return commensurate with the risks and his alternative use of his funds in alternative investments (opportunity cost). In our example, the calculation of payback reveals a relatively short exposure of funds and cash flow continuing beyond the payback period. It is interesting information in overall project evaluation, but it is not conclusive. Our model will automatically throw off payback as a by-product as we calculate the crucial time-adjusted NPV of the investment and DCF-ROR.

A version of cash payback is the cash bailout method. This approach takes into account not only the annual cash flow as shown in Figure A-2 but also the estimated liquidation value of the assets at the end of each year. If the liquidation value of a highly specialized project is zero, then cash payback and cash bailout are the same. But if it is assumed in our example that the liquidation value of the investment at the end of year 1 will be $275, the cash bailout would be one year (cash flow $225 plus liquidation value $275 = $500 original cash commitment).

We consider NPV as described a valid basis for determining the economic consequence of an investment decision. Many business economists use it as their sole criterion for the go–no-go decision for investment. We recognize this method as paramount throughout our analysis but prefer using it in conjunction with other measures rather than as the sole criterion.

CALCULATING RATE OF RETURN

We are now ready to examine the concept of DCF-ROR. It is completely different from the return on investment (ROI) commonly used in business. The conventional ROI is computed for an accounting period, generally on the accrual book figure; investment is taken at original cost, although it is sometimes taken at half original cost; no adjustment is made for time value when looked at in the long run.

We are talking about a very different ROR on investment: The DCF-ROR is the interest rate that discounts a project's net cash flow to zero present value. Let us expand Figure A-2, which shows a $60 NPV when a discount factor of 10 percent is used, to Figure A-3, which adds a discount factor of 18 percent and yields a $0 NPV.

The DCF-ROR is 18 percent. By definition, the DCF-ROR is the rate of return on the project determined by finding the interest rate at which the sum of the stream of aftertax cash flows, discounted to present worth, equals the cost of the project. Or, stated

Figure A-3. Arithmetic of determining DCF rate of return.

Year	Cash Flow	PV of $1 @ 10%	Discounted Cash Flow	PV of $1 @ 18%	Discounted Cash Flow
0	$(500)	1.000	$(500)	1.000	$(500)
0–1	225	.952	214	.915	206
1–2	225	.861	194	.764	172
2–3	150	.779	117	.639	96
3–4	50	.705	35	.533	26
TOTAL	$ 150		$ 60 NPV		$ 0 NPV

another way, the ROR is the maximum constant rate of interest the project could pay on the investment and break even. How was the 18 percent determined? By trial and error.

Many analysts use the NPV method exclusively; some use the DCF-ROR; others use the two methods to complement each other. Using NPV, positive or negative dollar values are determined with the cost of capital as the benchmark. Excess dollar PV is evaluated and a judgment is made. The DCF-ROR approach ignores the cost of capital in the calculation and determines what the ROR is on the total cash flow. The result of this approach on our example is to convert the $60 NPV into a percentage. It works out to 8 percent on top of the 10 percent that had been calculated for the NPV. Many businesspeople prefer working with the single figure of 18 percent for evaluating a project against a known cost of capital, instead of describing a project as having an NPV of $60 over the cost of capital. The two methods complement each other, and under certain circumstances one may give a better picture than the other.

Let us reexamine this special DCF-ROR to see what distinguishes it from the conventional ROR. It is time-adjusted to base year 0, so that all dollars are on a common denominator basis; it is calculated absolutely on a cash flow basis; the investment is a definite time-adjusted value; the ROR is determined at a single average rate over the total life of the investment. Certain implications of this statement require explanation.

The DCF-ROR is calculated over the full life of the project, and the accountant's yearly ROI cannot be used to test the success/failure of the new investment. If the planned life of a project is ten years, and if it can be segregated from other facets of the operation, the DCF-ROR has meaning only when the full economic life of the project is completed. However, in this case it is possible to monitor results on a year-to-year basis by examining the actual dollar cash flow and comparing it with the projected cash flow.

The one thing that disturbs business managers most with the DCF-ROR concept is the underlying mathematical assumption that all cash flows are reinvested immediately and constantly at the same rate as that which yields an NPV of 0. In our example in Figure A-3, 18 percent was used as the discount factor as a constant. Another case could just as easily have indicated a 35 percent ROR, with the implicit assumption that the cash flow was reinvested at 35 percent. But if the earning experience indicates a cost of capital of 10 percent, how can we reconcile the assumption that we can continue to earn 35 percent on the incremental flow?

Even though a company's average earnings reflect a cost of capital of 10 percent, the demands on incremental new investment may well have to be 18 to 35 percent to compensate for investments that fail to realize projected earnings. Opportunities to invest at 18 percent or 35 percent are not inconsistent with the average earnings of 10 percent. However, if it is felt that a projected rate of return of 18 percent, in our example, is a once-in-a-lifetime windfall and no new opportunities can be found to exceed the average 10 percent rate, then we are in trouble with our DCF-ROR concept. The reinvestment rate will not stand up. In this situation we have to combine both NPV and ROR to explain the situation in this way: The 10 percent ROR of this project covers the opportunity cost of money and throws off an additional $60 cash flow. If other projects of the same magnitude can be found so that the total cash flow generated can be reinvested at the same rate, there would actually be an ROR on the project of 18 percent (the DCF-ROR). The lack of other good investment opportunities is a constraint on the full earning capacity of the project.

We have examined three methods of evaluating investment opportunities. Cash payback evaluates money at risk. Present value measures the ability to cover the opportunity cost of an investment on a time-adjusted basis of money and indicates by an NPV whether the project under consideration will yield a "profit" or a "loss." The DCF-ROR is an extension of the NPV concept and translates it into a single ROR that, when compared with the opportunity cost of capital, gives a valid basis for evaluation.

Since NPV and DCF-ROR concepts take into account the opportunity cost of capital through the discounting technique, it may be stated as a principle that all projects under consideration where this opportunity cost is covered should be accepted. This proposition is both theoretically and practically sound, but three factors need to be considered: How do you determine the minimum acceptable ROR (the opportunity cost of capital) to select the proper discounting factor? How can you assume no constraints on the supply of capital so that all worthwhile projects can be accepted? How do you take risk into account when examining indicated results? These questions are examined in the next three sections.

USING COST-OF-CAPITAL GUIDELINES

How do you determine the minimum acceptable ROR (cost of capital) used in discounting? The cost of capital concept used here is not the same as the cost of borrowing. This is probably the most critical factor in the evaluation process. It is a unique and personal rate to each company. There is no guide to look to in other companies. Two companies looking at a potential investment, say an acquisition, may place two completely different values on it. To Company A, with a minimum required ROR of 10 percent, the investment could be attractive, while to Company B, with a required ROR of 25 percent, the investment would be totally unacceptable. The difference is centered in the cost of capital to each company, its opportunity ROR—the rate that can be expected on alternative investments having similar risk characteristics. An example of the arithmetic involved in reaching this conclusion can be seen when we modify Figure A-2 to include both a 10 percent and 25 percent discount factor and assume that both Companies A and B are the sole potential bidders for an investment with an asked price of $500 and a net cash flow of $150 (see Figure A-4).

The investment is very attractive to Company A but completely unacceptable to Company B—it would realize less than its objective of 25 percent. If Company A were in a position to know the cost of capital of Company B, it would know that Company B would not bid at all for this investment. Company A would know that it would be the sole bidder.

If a company has successfully earned 25 percent on the capital employed in it, an investment opportunity, to be attractive, would have to yield at least that rate. The 25 percent represents the cost of capital to that company, and an investment opportunity offering only 15 percent would be rejected. A second company with a

Figure A-4. Comparison of NPV using 10 percent and 25 percent discount factors.

		(A)		(B)	
Year	Cash Flow	PV of $1 @ 10%	Discounted Cash Flow	PV of $1 @ 25%	Discounted Cash Flow
0	$(500)	1.000	$(500)	1.000	$(500)
1	225	.952	214	.885	199
2	225	.861	194	.689	155
3	150	.779	117	.537	81
4	50	.705	35	.418	21
TOTAL	$ 150		$ 60 NPV		$ (44) NPV

10 percent cost of capital would find the same 15 percent potential attractive and accept it. Thus the same 15 percent opportunity investment is attractive to one and unattractive to the other. Both companies analyzing the identical situation reach different logical conclusions.

Cost of capital is *always* considered to be the combined cost of equity capital and permanent debt. We evaluate economic success/failure of a project without regard to how it is financed. Yet we know that money available for investment is basically derived from two sources: debt, with its built-in tax saving so that its cost is half the market price for money (assuming a 50 percent tax rate), and equity, which has as its cost the opportunity cost of capital of the owners.

It is necessary at times to break down the combined cost of capital into its components of cost of debt capital and cost of equity capital to put it in terms understandable to the businessperson who commonly measures results in terms of return on equity. To illustrate this cost of capital concept, we will assume that a corporation is owned by a single individual whose investment objectives are clearly defined. The total capitalization of the company is $100, made up of $30 permanent debt capital and $70 owner's equity capital. If preferred stock was outstanding at a fixed cost, it would be treated the same as debt. The aftertax interest rate of the debt money is 2.75 percent. The aftertax dollar return on the combined debt and equity capital of $100 under various operations would appear as shown in Figure A-5.

To restate these dollars as rates of return on the investment of $100, $30 debt, and $70 equity, the percentage return on capital would be as shown in Figure A-6.

If the company has been earning an average of $10 on the total investment of $100, and the cost of debt is $.825, the earning on owner's equity is $9.175. Stated as a rate of return, the $10 earned on $100 is 10 percent return on the total investment (combined cost of capital), and because of the leverage built into the capital structure with long-term debt, the $9.175 earning on equity yields a return on equity of 13.11 percent (cost of equity capital). When there is a 30 percent debt structure and the average cost of debt is 2.75 percent after taxes, we can readily convert return

Figure A-5. Aftertax dollar income on investment of $100.

Income on Total Investment (Before Interest)	$30 Debt × 2.75% Cost of Debt Capital	$70 Equity Income on Owner's Equity
$ 8.00	$0.825	$ 7.175
9.00	0.825	8.175
10.00	0.825	9.175
11.00	0.825	10.175
12.00	0.825	11.175

Figure A-6. Aftertax rate of return on investment of $100.

Rate of Return	Cost of Debt Capital	Rate of Return on Owner's Equity
8%	2.75% ($0.825 ÷ $30)	10.25% ($7.175 ÷ $70)
9	2.75	11.68
10	2.75	13.11
11	2.75	14.54
12	2.75	15.96

on total investment into return on equity by reading our table. It is quite simple to create similar tables for each company and its debt/equity ratio (e.g., with a 50/50 ratio and debt cost of 2.75 percent, a 10 percent return on total investment yields a 17.45 percent return on equity capital). If there is the opportunity to invest the company funds in alternative situations or reinvest the funds in the business and continue to earn at least 10 percent on the combined debt/equity funds, we would describe this as the opportunity cost of capital. This is the critical rate used in discounting: The discount rate used to determine NPV and the benchmark for comparing DCS-ROR are based solely on the combined cost of capital. The ROR to the stockholders can be derived and compared with their opportunity cost, that is, the ability to invest their funds elsewhere and earn at least the same rate.

EVALUATING PROFIT PROJECTS

Evaluating components of an investment program for a company is complex at any time. There are many categories of investment: (1) revenue-producing projects, (2) supporting facilities projects, (3) supporting services projects, (4) cost-savings projects, and (5) investments required to comply with public authority that will yield no return. Each must be evaluated to determine its incremental consequence.

When a project is isolated from the rest of the operation, evaluation is relatively clear. But sometimes a planned major investment embraces several auxiliary projects which, evaluated by themselves, are not very meaningful. When this occurs, it is necessary to construct a master model that includes all of the projects. Some of the auxiliary projects may not come into being for several years after the main investment is made, and may or may not produce a new positive cash flow. The master model in simple form may take on the appearance shown in Figure A-7 if individual projects of the types (a), (b), and (c) above are assumed (the figures do not add up—only format is demonstrated).

If the three projects are interrelated, they should be projected

Figure A-7. Master project.

Project	NPV	0	1	2	3	4	5	. . .	15
(a)	100	(30)	(2)	14	14	13	13		40
(b)	40	—	—	(15)	5	5	5		20
(c)	(26)	—	(2)	(2)	(4)	(4)	(4)		(10)
TOTAL	114	(30)	(4)	(3)	15	14	14		(50)

as a single entity. In our example, (a) is assumed to be a major facility that to be successful needs (b) added in three years as supporting facilities; (b) would have no basis for existence if (a) were not created. Project (c) may possibly be identified as a new computer/information system that will produce only costs, but would not exist if (a) and (b) were not created. All costs and all benefits for all corollary investments need to be projected as far into the future as possible to get a true evaluation. Investment evaluations that are made of a project with all the certainty of a DCF percentage can be grossly misleading if the supporting investment of satellites is not taken into account. Actually, these are not separate investments. There is only one—Project abc. The evaluation has to be of the new single entity. The postaudit can be of only the conglomerate single entity (abc).

Projects of the cost-savings category are generally easiest to identify and evaluate. There are relatively clear-cut choices: Invest $40,000 today for new labor-saving machines that will reduce labor costs $12,000 per year; the machines will last eight years, and quality of performance will be unchanged. Determine the NPV and/or DCF-ROR and accept/reject. Such investment opportunities constantly arise, but it is almost impossible to project them as part of a master project. As a result, such investments are evaluated as isolated investment opportunities that may occur in three years, or eight years, or never. When they occur, if of major proportions, they affect the potential return on the total investment.

A cost-incurring project, such as spend $100,000 to prevent air pollution or be closed up, is one of the few black-and-white decisions a manager faces. Ideally it would be expensed. It may have to be capitalized and written off and in addition have annual related operating expenses. This nondiscretionary investment falls into the same general category as a support project. The cash flow is always negative and must be included as an integral part of the master investment. A large enough commitment may sharply reduce the original projection, and a revision may be necessary.

On the basis of the techniques for evaluating planned capital investment, it is now possible to move to the methods of selecting among projects. As noted previously, in theory, selecting among projects is easy. Invest in anything that, when discounted at the appropriate marginal rate, will yield a positive NPV. Practically, for many reasons, there are constraints on capital in the minds of most managers. Let us look at the project selection problems that are involved for projects under consideration in a particular risk category when there is a limit on capital.

We have selected the NPV method as the best approach to analyze proposed projects of varying lives. Comparing projects under the DCF-ROR method can be misleading because of the different life factor and the reinvestment factor inherent in each ROR. Excess NPV avoids this difficulty. When the various projects are converted into a profitability index, selection is further facilitated. The profitability index is the ratio of the NPV to investment. For example:

$$\frac{\text{Present value of expected benefits}}{\text{Investment}} = \frac{\$132,000}{\$100,000} = 1.32$$

In selecting projects when a limit is imposed upon the amount available for investment, we look for the combination that will maximize combined NPV without exceeding the imposed limit. We know that we have reached this goal when we can no longer increase the combined NPV by substituting one project for another and still satisfy the constraint.

A way to achieve a satisfactory combination of projects is through trial and error. As a guide, we can use the profitability index (see Figure A-8). However, such ratios are not foolproof. This is illustrated where there are three possible projects requiring a total of $1,500 in initial outlays, but where $1,000 is the imposed limit.

Figure A-8. Profitability index.

Project	Net Present Value	[÷]	Investment: Cash Outlay	[=]	Profit-ability Index
A	$1,000		$600		1.67
B	700		500		1.40
C	500		400		1.25

   The choice is between investment in A + C (cash outlay $1,000) or investment in B + C (cash outlay $900). Since A + C have a combined greater NPV than B + C ($1,500 vs. $1,200), A + C should be selected even though C's ratio (1.25) is less than B's ratio (1.40). Such differences are common. The profitability index must always be used judiciously. When there are numerous projects to choose among, the combining process becomes more difficult.

Appendix B

HOW CUSTOMER MANAGERS MAKE LEASE-VS.-BUY DECISIONS

Ownership may be effected through outright purchase without indebtedness, through financed purchase, or, for all practical purposes, through a long-term lease. In an outright purchase, the buyer has full rights of ownership. Where the buyer obtains financing (before or after the purchase), his ownership is diminished by the limitations on his control of the asset. For example, in an installment purchase, the buyer's right to sell may be restricted by the lender's lien. In a long-term lease, the lessee lacks not only the right to sell but also all of the asset's residual rights, except for any purchase options available.

Short-term leasing is an alternative to the above forms of ownership. Here, the lessee is freed of almost all the risks of ownership, including obsolescence and maintenance, but the amount of the rental naturally reflects these advantages. In choosing between some form of ownership (as described above) on the one hand and short-term leasing on the other, management is faced with such *operational* considerations as maintenance, risk of obsolescence, and the degree of control desired. If ownership is selected, a further decision—this one involving essentially *financial* considerations—is necessary with regard to the form of ownership. It is with this second, basically more complex, decision that this appendix is concerned. The focus will be specifically on the choice between outright purchase and long-term lease as a form of ownership.

CHOOSING OUTRIGHT PURCHASE VS. LONG-TERM LEASE

The decision to buy or lease can be made only after a systematic evaluation of the relevant factors. The evaluation must be carried out in two stages: First, the advantages and disadvantages of purchase or lease must be considered, and second, the cash flows under both alternatives must be compared.

Figure B-1 shows the principal advantages and disadvantages of leasing from both the lessor's and lessee's standpoint. This listing is only a guide. For both parties, the relative significance of the advantages and disadvantages depends on many factors. Major determinants are a company's size, financial position, and tax status. For example, to a heavily leveraged public company, the disadvantage of having to record additional debt may be considerable, even critical; the disadvantage may be insignificant to a privately held concern.

ANALYZING CASH FLOWS

A cash-flow analysis enables the potential lessee to contrast his cash position under both buying and leasing. This is essentially a capital budgeting procedure, and the method of developing and comparing cash flows should conform to the company's capital budgeting policies and practices. There are several comparison criteria in current use, among which the three most common are rate of return, discounted cash flow, and net cash position.

1. *Outright purchase.* The cash outflows in an outright purchase are the initial purchase price or, assuming the asset is purchased with borrowed funds, as is almost always the case, the subsequent principal and interest on the loan. There will also be operating expenses, such as maintenance and insurance, but these

Figure B-1.   Leasing advantages and disadvantages.

Lessee Advantages

- *One hundred percent financing of the cost of the property (the lease is based on the full cost) on terms that may be individually tailored to the lessee.*
- *Possible avoidance of existing loan indenture restrictions on new debt financing.* Free of these restrictions, the lessee may be able to increase his base, as lease obligations are generally not reflected on the balance sheet, although the lease obligation will probably require footnote disclosure in the financial statements. (It should be noted, however, that a number of the more recent loan indentures restrict lease commitments.)
- *General allowability of rental deductions for the term of the lease, without problems or disputes about the property's depreciable life.*
- *Possibly higher net book income during the earlier years of the basic lease term than under outright ownership.* Rental payments in the lease's earlier years are generally lower than the combined interest expense and depreciation (even on the straight-line method) that a corporate property owner would otherwise have charged in the income statement.
- *Potential reduction in state and city franchise and income taxes.* The property factor, which is generally one of the three factors in the allocation formula, is reduced.
- *Full deductibility of rent payment.* This is true notwithstanding the fact that the rent is partially based on the cost of the land.

Lessee Disadvantages

- *Loss of residual rights to the property upon the lease's termination.* When the lessee has full residual rights, the transaction cannot be a true lease; instead, it is a form of financing. In a true lease, the lessee may have the right to purchase or renew, but the exercise of these options requires payments to the lessor after the full cost of the property has been amortized.
- *Rentals greater than comparable debt service.* Since the

(continues)

237

Figure B-1. (Continued)

---

lessor generally borrows funds with which to buy the asset to be leased, the rent is based on the lessor's debt service plus a profit factor. This amount may exceed the debt service that the lessee would have had to pay had he purchased the property.

- *Loss of operating and financing flexibility.* If an asset were owned outright and a new, improved model became available, the owner could sell or exchange the old model for the new one. This may not be possible under a lease. Moreover, if interest rates decreased, the lessee would have to continue paying at the old rate, whereas the owner of the asset could refinance his debt at a lower rate.

- *Loss of tax benefits from accelerated depreciation and high interest reductions in early years.* These benefits would produce a temporary cash saving if the property were purchased instead of leased.

Lessor Advantages

- *Higher rate of return than on investment in straight debt.* To compensate for risk and lack of marketability, the lessor can charge the lessee a higher effective rate—particularly after considering the lessor's tax benefits—than the lessor could obtain by lending the cost of the property at the market rate.

- *The lessor has the leased asset as security.* Should the lessee have financial trouble, the lessor can reclaim a specific asset instead of having to take his place with the general creditors.

- *Retention of the property's residual value upon the lease's termination.* The asset's cost is amortized over the basic lease term. If, upon the lease's expiration, the lessee abandons the property, the lessor can sell it. If the lessee renews or purchases, the proceeds to the lessor represent substantially all profit.

Lessor Disadvantages

- *Dependence upon lessee's ability to maintain payments on a timely basis.*
- *Vulnerability to unpredictable changes in the tax law that*

(1) reduce tax benefits and related cash flow or (2) significantly extend depreciable life. The latter measure would lessen the projected return upon which the lessor based his investment.

- *Probable negative after-tax cash flow in later years.* As the lease progresses, an increasing percentage of the rent goes toward nondeductible amortization of the principal. Both the interest and depreciation deductions (under the accelerated method) decline as the lease progresses.

- *Potentially large tax on disposition of asset imposed by the Internal Revenue Code's depreciation recapture provisions.*

---

items are excluded from the comparison because they will be the same under both purchase and leasing, assuming a net lease. The charge for depreciation is a noncash item. Cash inflows are the amount of the loan, the tax benefit from the yearly interest and depreciation, and the salvage value, if any.

2. *Leasing.* The lessee's cash flows are easier to define than the buyer's. The lessee pays a yearly rental, which is fully deductible. The lessee will thus have level annual outflows offset by the related tax benefit over the lease period. Salvage or residual value does not enter the picture because the lessee generally has no right of ownership in the asset. Figure B-2 is a comparison of cash flows developed under both buying and leasing.

3. *Comparing the cash flows.* Once the annual cash flows from outright purchase and leasing have been developed, the next step is to contrast the flows by an accepted method (such as discounted cash flow) to determine which alternative gives the greater cash benefit or yield. In so doing, some consideration must be given to the effects of changes in the assumptions adopted. Examples could include a lengthening by the IRS of the depreciation period or a change in interest rates. In this manner, a series of contingencies could be introduced into the analysis, as follows: Assume a ten-year life and a borrowing at 10 percent. If outright purchase is better by x dollars, then:

- A two-year increase in depreciable life reduces the benefit of outright purchase to $(x - y)$ dollars.

Figure B-2. Buying vs. leasing: a comparison of cash flows.

	Buy								Lease			
Period	Debt Service (a)	Principal Repayment	Interest Payment	Depreciation (b)	Interest Plus Depreciation	Tax Benefit at 50 Percent	Aftertax Cash Cost	Cumulative Aftertax Cash Cost	Rental (c)	Tax Benefit at 50 Percent	Aftertax Cash Cost	Cumulative Aftertax Cash Cost
1	$ 11,507	$ 3,614	$ 7,893	$ 12,500	$ 20,393	$10,197	$ 1,310	$ 1,310	$ 10,990	$ 5,495	$ 5,495	$ 5,495
2	11,507	3,912	7,595	11,667	19,262	9,631	1,876	3,186	10,990	5,495	5,495	10,990
3	11,507	4,234	7,273	10,833	18,106	9,053	2,454	5,640	10,990	5,495	5,595	16,485
4	11,507	4,583	6,924	10,000	16,924	8,462	3,045	8,685	10,990	5,495	5,495	21,980
5	11,507	4,961	6,546	9,167	15,713	7,856	3,651	12,336	10,990	5,495	5,495	27,475
6	11,507	5,370	6,137	8,333	14,470	7,235	4,272	16,608	10,990	5,495	5,495	32,970
7	11,507	5,813	5,694	7,500	13,194	6,597	4,910	21,518	10,990	5,495	5,495	38,465
8	11,507	6,292	5,215	6,667	11,882	5,941	5,566	27,084	10,990	5,495	5,494	43,960
9	11,507	6,810	4,697	5,833	10,530	5,265	5,242	33,326	10,990	5,495	5,495	49,455
10	11,507	7,372	4,135	5,000	9,135	4,567	6,940	40,266	10,990	5,495	5,495	54,950
11	11,507	7,979	3,528	4,167	7,695	3,848	7,659	47,925	10,990	5,495	5,495	60,445
12	11,507	8,637	2,870	3,333	6,203	3,101	8,406	56,331	10,990	5,495	5,495	65,940
13	11,507	9,349	2,158	2,500	4,658	2,329	9,178	65,509	10,990	5,495	5,495	71,435
14	11,507	10,120	1,387	1,667	3,054	1,527	9,980	75,489	10,990	5,495	5,495	76,930
15	11,507	10,954	553	833	1,386	693	10,814	86,303	10,990	5,495	5,495	82,425
	$172,605	$100,000	$72,605	$100,000	$172,605	$86,302 (d)	$86,303		$164,850	$82,425	$82,425 (e)	

NOTES

(a) $100,000 of debt borrowed at 8%. The debt service, payable quarterly in arrears, will be sufficient to amortize the loan fully over 15 years. (b) Asset cost of $100,000 will be depreciated over 15 years using the sum-of-the-years method. It was assumed that the asset had no salvage value. (c) Rental on a 15-year lease will be payable quarterly in arrears. The rental was based on an interest factor of 7¼%. It was assumed that the lessee's credit would require 8% interest. Since the lessor retains the depreciation benefits of the asset, he can charge a rent based on 7¼% even though he has financed the acquisition at 8%. (d) Present worth of $86,302 cost of buying, at 8%, is $41,198. (e) Present worth of $82,425 cost of leasing, at 8%, is $47,034.

Comment on notes (d) and (e). When comparing the cumulative aftertax cash costs, buying is the more expensive alternative by about $4,000. However, present valuing the annual outflows results in buying's being the most economical alternative by approximately $6,000.

- An upward change in interest rate reduces the benefit of outright purchase to $(x - z)$ dollars.

Probabilities could be assigned to the contingencies; for example, that the depreciable life could be extended by two years, 30 percent; or that interest rates could rise by one half a percentage point, 10 percent. Once the contingencies have been quantified, an overall probability of achieving the expected saving can then be calculated.

It must be stressed that the rate of return—the product of the cash-flow analysis—is not the exclusive or even, in some cases, the main determinant in deciding whether to buy or lease. Such factors as impact on financial statements, desire for operational flexibility, and loan restrictions, as well as other accounting, tax, economic, and financial considerations, may be collectively at least as important. These aspects are essentially nonquantitative, but they can be evaluated with a satisfactory degree of accuracy by weighing the advantages and disadvantages.

CONSIDERING TAXES

There are two ways in which a lease can be treated for tax purposes: as a true lease or as a form of financing. If the lease is viewed as a true lease, the lessee is entitled to a deduction, in the appropriate period, for his annual rental expenses. (Normally, the appropriate period is the period in which the liability for rent is incurred, in accordance with the terms of the lease, granted that the timing of the liability is not unreasonable.) If the lease is viewed as a form of financing, the lessee is deemed the property's equitable owner and is thus permitted to deduct the depreciation and interest expense.

The test the IRS applies to determine whether a lease is a true lease or a form of financing is basically an evaluation of the purchase options. If the lessee can purchase the property for less than the fair market value or for an amount approximately equal to what the debt balance would have been had the asset been bought outright, the transaction is viewed as a financing agreement. If the lessee has a purchase option in an amount substantially exceeding the probable fair market value or the debt balance, the transaction would probably be recognized as a lease.

Protecting the Business Relationship

A final aspect of the lease-buy decision relates to the lessor-lessee relationship. If the lessor encounters financial difficulties, under certain circumstances the prospective lessee can be adversely affected. That is, depending upon the terms of the lease and the lessor's financing arrangements, a lender might look to the property to satisfy a default by the lessor. Although careful wording of the agreement can afford a measure of protection, it is essential that the lessee look into the prospective lessor's financial condition, business reputation, and client relationships. If the findings are favorable, negotiations may be carried out with a minimum of delay and expense. If the findings are unfavorable, the prospective lessee might still wish to proceed, relying on the protective clauses in the agreement, or he might abandon the lease (at least with that party) entirely.

Index